NatWest Business Handbooks

This series has been written by a team of authors who all have many years' experience and are still actively involved in the day-to-day problems of the small business.

If you are running a small business or are thinking of setting up your own business, you have no time for the general, theoretical and often inessential detail of many business and management books. You need practical, readily accessible, easy-to-follow advice which relates to your own working environment and the problems you encounter. The NatWest Business Handbooks fulfil these needs.

- They concentrate on specific areas which are particularly problematic to the small business.
- They adopt a step-by-step approach to the implementation of sound business skills.
- They offer practical advice on how to tackle problems.

The author

Alan West owns and runs his own business and acts as a non-executive director in two others. He also serves as a consultant to several groups involved in the development of small businesses.

Other titles in this series

Book-keeping and Accounting
Computerisation in Business
Employing and Managing People
Exporting
Financial Control
Franchising
Health and Safety
Law for Small Businesses
Managing Growth
Marketing Decisions
Purchasing for Profit
Running a Shop
Selling
Small Business Finance
Small Business Survival
Starting Up
Taxation
Understanding VAT

NatWest Business Handbooks

A Business Plan

Alan West

Pitman

Pitman Publishing
128 Long Acre, London WC2E 9AN
A Division of Longman Group UK Limited

First published in Great Britain 1988
Reprinted in association with the National Westminster Bank,
1988 (twice), 1989, 1990
Reprinted in NatWest Business Handbooks series, 1991

British Library Cataloguing in Publication Data
Available on request from the British Library

ISBN 0 273 036289

The information in this book is intended as a general guide based upon the legislation at the time of going to press. Neither the Bank, its staff or the author can accept liability for any loss arising as a result of reliance upon any information contained herein and readers are strongly advised to obtain professional advice on an individual basis.

Typeset by Avocet Marketing Services, Bicester, Oxon.
Printed and bound in Great Britain by
Richard Clay Ltd, Bungay, Suffolk

To my mother,
for tolerance

Contents

Preface

You're in business, and you don't have to worry about the future?

This book is about a process that should be central to all businesses and is regrettably peripheral to most: the sitting down and planning for the future.

Your business may be a success, but will such successes continue?

In this book we introduce techniques which show how a business can understand what it is doing and how it can perform better. The book demonstrates how the information available about the small company can be used to the maximum effect. By setting a series of guidelines we shall see how a business manager can take the current company structure and develop from it a framework for the future and a means by which problems can be immediately identified.

So you like working twenty-four hours a day for the bank and the taxman?

This book examines methods of working more efficiently and more profitably.

You never thought business would be like this?

For the manager, running a small business often means being the jack of all trades and master of none. He or she will not have access to large professional staffs. This book outlines the areas that need to be considered.

In dealing with the basic principles underlying business planning, this book has been strongly influenced by the special needs of three groups of people.

- It is designed to help the business manager working in a small company to cope with some of the practical management problems that arise in the often haphazard operating environment of such enterprises – a special concern here is to aid the long-term profitable development of a successful business operation;
- It is designed to help the individual thinking about starting up a small business with the planning issues that must be considered;
- It is designed to help the business student in need of a methodical

approach to the creation of a business plan and a treatment of the problems in small business development.

The text contains:

- a structured approach to building up a business plan, with practical advice on marketing, production and financial control;
- a method by which progress in the business can be monitored and controlled;
- a guide to how to present these plans to funding organizations or individuals.

Guidelines are supplied on how those involved should be thinking about the special problems of small business, and how other companies have faced and dealt with similar problems. The book presents a simple, self-help approach which can be applied systematically by the manager with no access to a planning department and can be shaped to the different requirements of the business: for the bank manager, local authorities, major shareholders and most important of all, himself or herself. No prior knowledge of marketing or economics is assumed.

By prompting answers to questions which the entrepreneur may never have considered, the development of a business plan should at the very least provoke thought about issues fundamental to a successful business. A plan is evolved in a step by step fashion with particular attention to the issues that will need to be resolved and the benefits such an approach will bring. We then go on to consider the problems of the small business and how the plan can be used as a control mechanism by which progress can be evaluated. A series of case studies based on real-life examples is also included.

In an appendix simple spreadsheet models are produced that can be used by the small business to analyse major elements of business performance: pricing, customer performance, profitability and cash flow – extremely important aspects of a successful business operation. These models enable the business to gain a more accurate control over those elements of the business environment most likely to cause business failure:

- poor pricing;
- failure to control cash flow;
- lack of proper funding for the business objectives;
- lack of clear goals either in the short- or long-term.

These models can be applied to any simple computer system using a spreadsheet package, or can be manually derived.

Clear thinking about where the business is going and how scarce but valuable assets can best be directed is probably more important for the small business with limited resources than it is for a larger organization. There is, nevertheless, a tendency for people to consider business planning as a preoccupation of the highly successful commercial enterprise and not to realize that the planning process is essentially an evolution from a simple statement to a complex corporate document.

Alan West

Acknowledgements

This book has developed as a result of many discussions with individuals involved with the small business community and I would like especially to thank Steve Birchell of Hackney Enterprise Agency and Steven Hutton of Greenwich Employment Development Unit for their comments.

I would like to thank Gower Publications for permission to use the Marginal Profitability and Competitive Bidding spreadsheet models from my book *Spreadsheet Marketing*.

1 Why a business plan?

The problems of small businesses □ The potential of small businesses □ Why is the business plan so important to the small business? □ The demands of business planning □ The limitations of business planning □ Planning and success – conclusion

People start businesses for many reasons: for profit, independence, or in desperation when faced with long-term unemployment.

Some small businesses are what dreams are made of: rags to riches progress of dazzling proportions. Apple Computers, for example, began in a garage and grew into a billion dollar corporation within five years. Polaroid, another American success story, showed similar growth. The American computer company, Compaq, has also shown this type of meteoric growth since its foundation in late 1981, becoming one of America's top 500 companies by the end of 1985 with profits topping $40 million. Successes of this nature are fewer in the United Kingdom but they are there: Amstrad, with its origins in the production of record sleeves, quickly became a major force in the UK hi-fi and home computer market; the furniture chain MFI increased earnings twenty-fold from 1960 to 1970, and financial groups like Slater Walker have showed spectacular rises followed by catastrophic falls.

Though these success stories are heartening to all entrepreneurs, showing as they do that there may indeed be gold at the end of the rainbow, the reality of the small business world is very different from the tantalizing success stories.

The problems of small businesses

The average small UK business can be regarded as viable if it merely survives the first five years of existence. Research shows that approximately eighty-five per cent of businesses fail in the first five years, with problems being most acute in the building, transport, light engineering and fashion industries.

Although the crucial problems will vary, government and other studies present a fairly clear picture of the nature and problems of a small business. Major difficulties facing the expanding small firm occur because of:

(a) problems of establishment in the first one or two years – finding customers, developing products;

(b) problems of consolidation in the next period – finding staff, delegating, controlling the business;

(c) problems of expansion in the next phase – finding finance, competing with much bigger firms in the market.

Because it is small, the company will continually have to overcome certain common problems:

- a limited number of employees;
- limited financial resources;
- a small management team primarily consisting of the partners in the business. These individuals will often be learning the main problems of the business as they go along;
- a fairly narrowly defined geographic and industry sector;
- premises that are unlikely to be totally suitable for the nature of the business conducted;
- reliance on historic information provided by external accountants which will generally be at least one year out-of-date.

Taken together these factors emphasize the fragility of the small business. For example, if a key member of the team quits the effect can be catastrophic; in a larger organization this would not matter. Should a substantial customer be slow in placing an order a crisis might result.

The major problems facing the small company can therefore be summarized as follows.

- Management will lack skills in a number of key areas. A company may be founded by an engineer who rapidly becomes faced with problems of finance, selling and promotion, which may easily lead the company into difficulties if not properly understood. The knowledge possessed by management of many of the key problems facing the company may therefore be limited.
- Management will lack time to carry out many of the complex tasks that the growing business will demand, and because of the limited financial resources will not be able to recruit staff to handle these problems. This is a common experience of many businesses, that management spend all their time 'fire-fighting', and do not pay sufficient attention to the necessary developmental aspects of the business.
- Management will react to problems rather than try to foresee them and plan to cope with them.
- In common with larger organizations, the employees of the company

are unlikely to be fully informed of the likely prospects for the firm, which may make the rapid change of direction, often essential in the small firm, difficult to achieve.

- Management information on which decisions can be based will be limited and this may hamper the use of the correct technology to resolve a particular problem.
- The small firm will tend to lack experience of developing outside the sector in which it is currently operating. The percentage of turnover that comes from export in small companies, for example, is generally less than one per cent.
- The close involvement of the owner in the business will often make objective judgement difficult.

These are the features which characterize the small business as one which muddles along from day to day. Rather than controlling its destiny, it allows itself to be controlled. The manager makes little or no attempt to plan ahead – to *manage* in other words. There is a general failure to appreciate that looking forward a little can be a very effective method of easing the problems of the present.

The potential of small businesses

Though one can paint a black picture of the viability of small enterprises, they do have a number of strengths over their larger competitors which can be effectively exploited.

- Decision-making can be rapid as structures are simple, and the business can change direction quickly to take advantage of altered market conditions.
- Once a decision is taken it can be implemented more rapidly and the results will be more readily apparent than in a more complex organization.
- Relations between staff and managers will tend to be more equitable and labour relations will not pose severe problems or hamper change. Communication with the staff will be fairly straightforward; working relationships will tend to be flexible, which should have a beneficial effect on staff morale as the working environment is generally more relaxed.
- There is potentially a much better working environment for staff who will be able to see the effects of personal effort clearly and quickly. This is an important motivating factor, especially for those staff who should be encouraged to put forward good ideas.
- Management will be close to the customer and the market, and will be able to react to changes in the market more rapidly because of this

knowledge. We are all aware of senior managers in the consumer goods sector who never go into a shop.

Why is the business plan so important to the small business?

Few companies are fortunate enough to operate in industries where they are without competition. In today's environment it will seem to small businesses that the bigger firms in the market enjoy most of the advantages, and that they must follow the famous adage of Avis 'We try harder', in order to survive.

The small business is very much in the position of the motorcycle in heavy traffic: by dodging and weaving it can move more quickly through the press of vehicles, though it is alarmingly vulnerable to being run over by heavy lorries!

While it is true that the small firm can operate on tighter profit margins than the large firm, doing so can be the equivalent of walking a tightrope: sound judgement is essential and there is no margin for error.

This underlines the particular problem of small businesses: *resource limitation* means that it is especially important that what is available is used to maximum effect. In other words the business must plan more effectively than others.

All businesses must take decisions about resource allocation and the large enterprise, which can absorb a certain amount of waste, uses a detailed business plan as a management control system. Although the problems of big business are quite different from those of an infant operation, clear goals are just as important. The planning process will be central to the solution of many of the problems that the small business faces.

- It will identify business areas that are not completely under control, to which managers have perhaps given inadequate attention and where action is essential.
- It will provide a framework through which employees and others can be informed of the company's future direction.
- It will force management to consider the future strategy of the firm; to weigh up the strengths and weaknesses in an objective fashion.
- It will demand that management information systems be improved, which will have benefits for all decision-making within the organization.
- It will identify key development areas for which the firm will need to develop expertise.

- It will provide the basis for analysing whether or not a new product or process will be a success, especially valuable in the development of short-term forecasts.
- It can be very useful in providing the information on the prospects of the company required by likely sources of finance. This is particularly important for increasing numbers of businesses which are dependent on external sources of finance such as bank loans or local government grants. Large organizations are generally far more successful in gaining access to finance, often because they are able to provide more detailed justification of their requirements.

Example

Mobility Ltd, a company in West London, had grown to a turnover of £300,000 in four years, with three activities, vehicle repair, leasing, and garage services. Near bankruptcy forced the company to re-evaluate its activities. It found that the vehicle repair side of the business was losing £70,000 per annum in a highly competitive market. Vehicle leasing was very profitable and faced weak competition. Garage services broke even over the year. Analysis showed that one area of the business was draining resources from another: corrective action allowed the company to move from a position of imminent collapse into healthy profit.

The demands of business planning

Preparing a business plan will make demands upon the organization, although the extent of this can be exaggerated. Thus it is too frequently assumed that business planning is too complex and expensive a process to have much relevance for a small business. To get worthwhile results, business planning in a large organization will indeed require considerable investment. In common with many activities the more the individuals put into the exercise initially, the greater the value, and the small business enjoys certain advantages over the larger which will help to control the cost of drawing up a business plan.

With fewer products or services to offer, fewer staff employed, and serving a more limited market, the small business can clarify its objectives far more easily than a larger organization for a more modest investment in time, money and data. There will, however, be for each organization a point at which further development of the planning process does not produce useful results – the point of diminishing returns.

Any plan must meet three criteria.

- It must be simple.
- It must be accurate.

- It must be useful.

The highly sophisticated planning system of the multinational company will require a vast collection of data which will lead to the loss of accuracy. It will demand complex computer analysis which will be carried out by staff removed from the day-to-day problems of implementation. It will often cost a great sum of money to build up and a similar sum each year to maintain.

The small to medium company neither has or needs these resources and must regard the planning function as another instance of investment and return. The more data that is collected, the greater the chances of error, the greater the cost and the greater the likelihood that the conclusions provided will be far from clear.

Part of the benefit of developing what will initially be a simple business plan and continuing to monitor it is the fact that shortfalls in information will be clearly identified and the limited capacity of the small firm to allocate resources to collecting information will be allowed for.

The limitations of business planning

There are things that a business plan cannot do.

- Planning is not a panacea. It does not allow management to escape from taking decisions; indeed it should help by clearly identifying the problem and the possible solutions.
- Planning should not be seen as a rigid unbending answer to all the firm's problems. External and internal conditions will change, and require an alteration in direction. To accommodate such factors larger companies organize reviews during the plan period. This may be feasible for some smaller businesses but less relevant to the one-man show. Yet even here, the discipline of noting down alterations helps to secure a degree of continuity and relevance within the plan.
- Planning is only as good as the people who carry it out and the use to which the plan is put.

Many firms go through the planning process as an annual ritual such as a thanksgiving service or local elections, vaguely interesting to watch but not particularly relevant to reality.

There is little point in planning if it is not realistic – larger firms may have time to play such games but the small firm cannot afford the luxury. A plan, once completed, should be the best possible solution to the conflicting problems that are facing the firm. As it has involved time and effort in preparation it should be *used* and not discarded at the earliest opportunity.

Example

Reggae Ltd, a firm starting to manufacture ethnic shampoo, changed financing arrangements, distribution methods, packaging designs, pricing structures and product list after carefully considering the market realities and how the company could become established. The final plan that evolved coherently integrated the demands of the market with the limited resources that the firm had available.

Planning and success — conclusion

Research in the United States on a large number of small companies shows that the stability of growth measured over a period of five to ten years is closely correlated with the amount of planning that the company carried out, i.e. the degree of awareness of how external and internal factors affect the future of the business. Short-term success does not appear to be greatly affected by the amount of planning that the business carries out, but good planning is fundamental to long-term profitable survival.

2 What is a business plan?

For what timescale is the business plan relevant? □ What are the plan objectives? □ How to draw up a business plan □ Some points to remember □ Who draws up the business plan?

A business plan is a systematic way of approaching future problems and overcoming them. It is not, however, a form of clairvoyance which will predict what will happen to the company in the future. In fact it is quite the opposite: it is an instrument of the present developed through trial and error and using the company's experience and achievement in the past to plot the way forward realistically. The plan will aim to achieve the most advantageous and workable compromise between what a company *wants* to do and what it *can* do. It will show the company how its proposed policies are integrated and how one issue affects another.

For what timescale is the business plan relevant?

The business plan will outline the necessary action that must be taken immediately, as well as issues that need to be considered in the medium- and long-term. For example, product and production issues might vary across a three-year period in the following fashion:

	Short	*Medium*	*Long*
Product	Maintain current	Develop variants	Diversify
Production	Extra shift	New equipment	New factory

Each of these elements will be linked with each other in different ways and demand varying levels of investment both in time and money if the desired result is to be achieved.

What are the plan objectives?

As stated in the preceding chapter, the plan must be:

- simple,
- accurate,
- useful.

We shall attempt to work to these parameters when carrying out the tasks involved in drawing up a plan for the small company.

The business planner will begin by seeking answers to the question:

- Where is the business at present?

The information gathered will supply a firm base which will help to supply answers to another important question:

- What objectives or goals should the business be trying to reach?

Knowledge of the current state of the business followed by the definition of goals will automatically lead the planner to ask:

- What is the most effective way of achieving these goals?

How to draw up a business plan

The planner must carry out a number of very specific tasks to make sure that the end document answers these three questions. They involve various steps which can be remembered by the mnemonic: **How Gainfully A Quiet Reflection Can Succeed.**

- History
- Goals
- Assumptions
- Quantification
- Resource allocation
- Checking
- Sensitivity analysis

History – Where is the business now?

A detailed examination of the business to assess what has happened over the previous year in certain key areas is an important element of business planning. It will involve considering the company's performance in such areas as selling, pricing, production, distribution and finance and administration.

In a small company the activities in some of these areas may not be very complex. Sometimes, in fact, they may on the surface appear too simple to merit attention. But it is only by ensuring that such seemingly straightforward areas are periodically reviewed, that we can assume that an operation that was simple in the past has continued to remain so.

The detailed examination of past business performance may also lead the planner to consider the targets the business has set itself in the past and whether it has achieved them.

The information required about the company's performance in the recent past will cover certain key areas:

(a) the product or services supplied;
(b) the industry (see Chapter 3);
(c) marketing (see Chapter 4);
(d) production (see Chapter 5);
(e) finance (see Chapter 6);
(f) personnel (see Chapter 7);
(g) administration (see Chapter 8).

Examining these facets of company activity will enable management to build up a picture of the strengths and weaknesses of the business. They are covered in greater detail in Part 2, where questions are asked about various aspects of the business and the answers are summarized in chart form at the end of the relevant chapter. This will identify for the planner those areas that require detailed consideration and will indicate any necessary changes in direction for the business.

Goals – Where does the business want to be?

The planner's key task concerns the clarification of what the business is trying to achieve. Because small businesses are so flexible it can happen that they change direction without managers being completely aware of this.

The detailed examination of the state of the business will provide some of the indications needed as to whether the firm should formally consider re-defining its goals. (See also Chapter 9.)

Assumptions – Are they correct?

Central to this task will be the definition of the assumptions on which the whole plan is based. You may, for example, consider that economic inflation is likely to continue at 5 per cent per annum or rise to 7 per cent – both would be realistic possibilities but each will have differing effects on such important elements of the business plan as pricing, costing, profit and cash flow. Similarly for the larger company with considerable export business the expectation of what the exchange rates will be over the length of the planning cycle will be extremely important.

It is good discipline to note down formally the assumptions that are involved – what may be self-evident to you will often appear as total and absolute nonsense to other individuals in the planning process. (See also Chapter 9.)

Quantification – How can objectives be expressed in financial terms?

Redefining and clarifying objectives is more than an exercise in juggling with words. The planner must translate these objectives into figures or targets to assess their likely impact on the financial status of the company.

Sales values net of (i.e. minus) production and administrative costs will provide cash flows and borrowing requirements. (See also Chapter 10.)

Resource allocation – How do we achieve objectives?

Once objectives have been set and their financial implications analysed, the planner will have to consider the actions and resources that need to be allocated to achieve these targeted figures. Will they, for example, require a re-organization of certain areas? Will the company need more advertising, or will it need to change the pattern of its advertising? (See also Chapter 10.)

Checking – Is the plan realistic?

The realistic plan will invariably involve cross-checking to minimize inconsistency and areas of conflict. When an operation is simple the chances of this happening are reduced, but even here the planner must check whether the way the available resources have been allocated are consistent with the overall objectives of the organization, and whether the objectives are feasible for the business. (See also Chapter 11.)

Sensitivity analysis – Is the plan flexible?

An additional cross-checking exercise will mean considering the effects which changes in some of the key assumptions will have on the outcome of the plan, i.e. how sensitive the outcome is to these changes. For example, what effect would the introduction or increase of VAT by the government have on the firm's products?

Another check takes the shape of re-defining the plan and re-allocating resources should the original plan fail to meet the objectives of the firm. (See also Chapter 11.)

Some points to remember

Commitment to preparing a business plan will use up resources, even if it is only staff time. To ensure that this effort is not wasted through the production of a useless end document, the firm carrying out a business analysis should bear a number of key factors in mind.

(a) *Objectivity*. To be workable the plan must be realistic; it must take account of all the shortcomings of the firm, and the limitations of the people involved. This will ensure that the plan is achievable with the resources available. No businessman or woman should ever deceive himself or herself about the likely future prospects. Verbal promises from individuals met at conventions, conferences, or over a drink in the local pub, rarely if ever become concrete business.

(b) *Assumptions*. Every plan will demand that the organization makes certain assumptions about the future. Some of these will be more important than others and it is vital that the key assumptions are clearly identified.

- It is important that where different people are involved in the preparation of a plan they must all use the same assumptions in the development of estimates, for example, that a common exchange rate or inflation rate is used.
- Such procedures will also identify the central assumptions that are essential to the smooth working of the plan.

(c) *Length of projection*. Many businesses have fixed ideas about the timescale that should be considered to forward plan accurately. There is no hard and fast rule, however, for the majority of organizations, but many businesses find that commitment to, and interest in, the business plan diminishes as the length of the forward projection increases, and individuals have to struggle with more and more complex calculations until the whole process becomes a rote exercise. A ten-year forecast is unlikely to be worth the paper it is printed on except as a broad strategic idea as to where business may be obtained.

For the average business a three-year projection will be adequate, with the following year in detail and the next two in outline. For fast moving industries with a high content of technology the planning horizon may be more limited, with two years or eighteen months being the longest that is feasible.

Each business will therefore need to determine the planning horizon relevant to its needs; a rapidly changing industry or high levels of investment will have different effects.

Who draws up the business plan?

Generally speaking the more accurate the information about the state of the business the stronger will be the position in drawing up a business plan. Judgements will be required and the ability to support them with hard facts will obviously improve the credibility of the end result.

Another very important method of improving the accuracy of the judgements involved is making sure that all the skills available within the company are used, not simply allocating the least useful member of staff to prepare the plan.

Any plan is only as good as the individuals that create it. The adage 'garbage in means garbage out' applies most of all to business planning.

Ultimately those employed by the business will assume some of the responsibility of implementing the plan effectively. It therefore makes sense to talk to those with detailed knowledge of different aspects of the company's operations and make sure that they contribute to the plan. If possible they could be asked to produce their detailed ideas about the future progress of the business. The number of people that can make such a contribution will naturally vary according to the size of the firm; it is, however, a good idea to cast the net as wide as possible as the more people that take part the more effective the plan, for several reasons.

- People can readily feel their jobs threatened by the concept of business efficiency. Consultation with employees in a business that has not had a business plan in the past should be seen as essential to creating positive attitudes towards the plan.
- More employees will feel involved in the future well being of the company.
- The larger the number of individuals involved the lower the chance that unworkable solutions will be arrived at. The corollary is that too much consensus can produce a conservative plan that is at odds with the objectives of the entrepreneurial small business manager. He or she will have to take account of this in the final overall compilation of the results.

The involvement of large numbers of individuals in the planning process can nevertheless create problems of integrating the data within a limited period of time – particularly if the planning horizon is five or ten years. Making one or two individuals responsible for the collection and integration of data will in these circumstances become essential, particularly if the plan is used on a computer as a management control mechanism.

Integration of plan data is only possible if a standard format is used for planning purposes, with common agreement on the assumptions underlying the plan.

Move on now to Chapters 3–8 where we examine the environment in which the business operates and look at various aspects of company activity, asking key questions about each. As noted earlier, planners will be able to use their answers to these key questions to highlight those areas which need action, gradually building up a complete picture of the business and its needs.

PART TWO CURRENT BUSINESS POSITION

3 The industry

The nature of the industry □ Industry size □ Size of market and market share □ Competitive structure □ Political and economic trends □ Technology and speed of change □ Forecasting sales □ Price trends/inflation □ Seasonality □ Trade fluctuations □ Government aid and assistance □ Research and development □ Trade information

An understanding of the industry is essential to business success; knowing how the industry considers new products, how it acquires information, how it is growing are all important to the developing firm. Some of the key questions that the firm needs to answer in this area are considered in this chapter.

The nature of the industry

1. Does the firm have a clear idea of the market in which it is operating?

Select one of the following, whichever is most appropriate, and enter the answer in the chart at the end of the chapter.

1	2	3	4	5
Very unclear	Unclear	Some	Clear	Very clear

Before the direction of a business can be defined it is essential to have a clear understanding of the industry and market in which the business is operating.

The Swiss watch industry is a clear example of manufacturers identifying accurately the market in which they operate. As cheap Japanese competition developed, the Swiss watch industry saw that what they were in fact selling was jewellery rather than precision time-keeping instruments. Improving the styling of their products has enabled them to continue to dominate the world market by value of product sold.

Similar exercises have been carried out in some small businesses.

- A large photographic studio correctly identified that it was also selling 'space' in addition to photographic work. Correctly identifying this asset enabled the company to generate large revenues from selling space for exhibitions and other events.
- A producer of plant pots saw that he was in the ornamental garden market rather than the container market.

A useful aid in identifying the company's real market is to consider the effects of substantially raising or lowering the price of the product or service that is offered. What other markets would this open for the company? What additional features would be necessary for the product in that sector of the market?

For example, a firm supplying specially equipped buses for the disabled identified the total disabled transport market including holiday travel as potential customers, rather than the narrow public service sector in which they were originally operating. A firm producing clothes, for example, could regard itself as being in the bespoke fabric business which might suggest that the firm could produce bed-linen, quilts, even soft toys. Similarly a firm involved in ship repair might find a useful market in historic ship repair, or even building ships for the TV and film industry.

Input for the business plan

Accurate identification of the real industry in which the firm operates is important in defining objectives and assessing the real competition the firm is facing.

Industry size

2. What is happening to the industry in which the firm is operating? Is it growing or declining? What are the expectations about it? Compared with last year, is turnover expected to decline, grow or remain static?
Compared with last year, is it:

Select one of the following, whichever is most appropriate, and enter the answer in the chart at the end of the chapter.

1	2	3	4	5
Down 5%	Down 1%–5%	Static	Up 1% –5%	Up 5%

It is fairly clear that all firms should try to establish themselves in industries that are growing. Declining industries show increasing excess production which inevitably affects prices, lowering overall profitability.

Input for the business plan

Companies must consider whether they should try to develop interests in an industry or sector with greater growth potential. Obviously this is more important if the answer to the question reveals that the company is operating in a declining sector.

Information on the size of the market may often be difficult to obtain. There are, however, a number of publications that can assist. They include:

- trade journals,
- government publications,
- research centres' publications, chambers of commerce and, in London, institutions such as the City Business Library.

Growing and declining markets demand different strategies. Growing markets demand:

- heavy investment in promotion to ensure trial and repeat purchase of the company's product compared with that of the competition;
- investment in research and development to widen the product range as growth flattens out;
- increasing investment in stocks and distribution to meet the growing demand;
- aggressively low competitive pricing during the early stages of market growth followed by increases as the market growth is reduced.

Declining markets in contrast demand:

- accurate control over promotional expenditure;
- a reduced product range;
- the maximum attention paid to the level of stocks and distribution costs;
- a pricing policy designed to maximize profitability rather than expand market share.

For many small companies a declining market may offer many opportunities as large companies will often withdraw from them. On the other hand, the citizen band radio and skateboard markets have recently provided examples of the need for companies to be extremely careful in declining markets, with many ensuing bankruptcies.

Size of market and market share

3. What is the current size of the market and the company's market share? Has the company acquired a greater market share over the past years or has its share declined? Compared with last year what changes have there been in the company's market share. Has market share declined or grown compared with last year?

Select one of the following, whichever is most appropriate, and enter the answer in the chart at the end of the chapter.

1	2	3	4	5
Declined by 3%	Declined by 1%	No change	Grown by 1%	Grown by 3%

As a company's market share increases, it will become progressively more difficult to increase sales. For example, the firm with 1 per cent market share may find it easy to double sales; for the firm with 55 per cent of the market it is patently impossible. Though research has shown that firms with high market shares tend to be more profitable than those with low shares, each firm will have to accept a limit to growth within each market sector. More serious will be a continuing decline in market share.

Input for the business plan

Large reductions in market share require corrective action. This will demand concentration on issues of distribution, product quality, product development, pricing and promotion.

Competitive structure

The nature and history of the industry's competitive structure will have an important influence on the strategy that the firm develops. This will be especially important should the competitive structure change which might, for example, occur when a major company enters the market or when a new product gains a major part of the market from its competitors. In each case the company will face problems or opportunities that must be accommodated in its plan.

In many industries the competition may be a far more important factor in developing the plan than the consumer.

4. Compared with last year has the competitive position changed?

Select one of the following, whichever is most appropriate, and enter the answer in the chart at the end of the chapter.

1	2	3	4	5
Very much	A lot	Some	A little	None

Each competitive position has a traditional response in business theory.

Market leaders

These companies will have to consider methods by which they will maintain their lead.

(a) *A continuing high level of product development* to prevent new entrants into the market.

(b) *Manufacturing economies of scale.* It is in the interests of market leaders to concentrate on large-scale production runs to maximize economies of production and ensure that the competition will not be able to match the unit price.

(c) *Strong continuing promotional activity.* Once a company establishes a strong position it is in its interests to keep the name of the company ahead of the competition. A good example of this has been the rise of Norfolk Farms – the high level of promotional expenditure has made it very difficult for other companies to become established in the frozen poultry and poultry products sector.

(d) *Tactical activity.* The market leader is able to use this position to maximize sales and restrict the market available to the competition by pricing, distribution, and sales promotional activity.

Market challengers

Market challengers will have strategies to enable them to erode the dominant position of the market leader(s).

(a) *Direct attack.* Market challengers can invest heavily to attempt to gain market share from market leaders. Such a policy tends to be both extremely expensive and ineffective. Companies with substantial funds such as the major multinationals can use this route to become established in the market: for the small firm it is unlikely to be effective.

(b) *Price reduction.* Though this is one of the easiest policies to follow it does create problems for the company that chooses to follow it. First, it inevitably reduces the profitability of the company compared with the competition. Secondly, it will have an effect on the perceptions of the market – cheap prices are often associated with low quality.

(c) *Product differentiation.* Finding a new market sector or developing specialized products can be an important method of enabling market followers to establish themselves eventually as a dominant force in the market.

(d) *Distribution changes.* New methods of distribution can effectively expand market share – direct mail instead of sale through traditional outlets may, for example, be a very viable option for a number of companies.

Market specialists

These by their very nature must carefully evaluate various strategies.

(a) *Production volumes.* Market specialists will need to monitor market trends carefully to ensure control of production volumes. Amstrad, the hi-fi and home computer company, for example, managed to determine the market trends for citizen band radio to a nicety, withdrawing from the market just as the peak was reached. This underlines the necessity of understanding the level of growth in the market mentioned earlier.

(b) *Pricing.* The specialist manufacturer will need close control over pricing especially if production runs are limited.

Commodity producers

Companies that act as commodity producers will need to concentrate on manufacturing efficiency to ensure that their contract work is profitably completed. Bibby Edible Oils has, for example, managed to produce a viable competitive cooking oil, Golden Fields, in the face of rising supermarket own-brands by concentrating on efficient production processes.

Input for the business plan

Defining the competitive position will be crucial for the business in deciding on practical objectives and producing the detailed plans that go with them. A computer software firm, for example, saw that product specialization was the only viable route in the face of domination of the industry by large groups. The company found for itself a profitable market niche in designing tailor-made systems for the oil industry.

Political and economic trends

5. How much of an idea has the company of the impact of political and economic trends upon the company's prospects?

Select one of the following, whichever is most appropriate, and enter the answer in the chart at the end of the chapter.

1	2	3	4	5
None	Little	Some	Good	Very good

For many companies political and economic trends will have significant effects.

- Unemployment levels will affect demand for many products or services.
- Changes in local government finance can affect some industries directly.

Input for the business plan

Political and economic trends should be one of the key assumptions that businesses should include in the business plan.

Legislative changes

6. What are the chances of legislative controls changing during the planning period?

Select one of the following, whichever is most appropriate, and enter the answer in the chart at the end of the chapter.

1	2	3	4	5
Very high	High	Neutral	Poor	Nil

Legislative changes can considerably affect a whole industry. For example, a reduction in local government spending through rate control measures, changes in equipment buying policy for schools, alterations in the regulations controlling imports, would all have considerable effects on firms engaged in certain sectors. Similarly, changes in the way that government allocates regional grant can have a significant impact on many manufacturing companies. Though it is unlikely that the government will reduce the level of administration that the firm is obliged to carry out, a change in VAT administration, for example, could mean that one or two fewer employees might be required in the accounts department. In the 1980s changes in farming support for milk products have meant disaster for many dairy farmers who have no other income.

Input for the business plan

One of the important assumptions that a firm needs to make is the question of likely major changes in legislation, and how the company should plan to minimize such effects.

Social change

7. How good an idea has the company of the likely changes in the social environment over the planning period?

Select one of the following, whichever is most appropriate, and enter the answer in the chart at the end of the chapter.

1	2	3	4	5
None	Little	Some	Good	Very good

Social change will affect some industries more than others, but change can be fairly rapid even in 'traditional' industries such as office furniture. Companies such as Binatone in the home electrical sector have successfully identified social trends by introducing low cost telephone answering machines, portable stereos, and a range of similar products.

Input for the business plan

Making assumptions about changes in social conditions over the planning period should at least be attempted – will social factors lead to an increase or decrease in demand?

Technology and speed of change

8. Does the nature of the product sold in the industry vary from year to year?

Select one of the following, whichever is most appropriate, and enter the answer in the chart at the end of the chapter.

1	2	3	4	5
Greatly	A lot	Some	Little	Nil

Each industry has its own pattern of change. The record and film industries live on a continually changing diet; butter making, in contrast, shows little change from year to year.

Input for the business plan

The company must outline the likely pattern of development that it will need to follow: what percentage of the turnover for the forthcoming year will have to come from new products? What implications will this have for the allocation of resources?

A technique used by major companies in an attempt to minimize the uncertainty caused by rapidly changing social, economic and technological factors is to ask all senior management involved in the business to provide on a questionnaire basis their ideas of likely trends. This attempts to remove the bias inherent in group planning sessions while achieving an overall consensus of the likely future trends and how they will affect the company.

Forecasting sales

9. How do you rate the ability of the company to define likely future sales?

Select one of the following, whichever is most appropriate, and enter the answer in the chart at the end of the chapter.

1	2	3	4	5
Very poor	Poor	Moderate	Good	Very good

The capacity to define future sales trends is a vital part of successful business planning. From it will flow all other factors in the business – production, financial and personnel requirements. Naturally the company will influence sales by a number of actions: changes in product quality, pricing, distribution, packaging and promotion will all have their effects. New product introductions are obviously more difficult to forecast accurately even for large companies: for example when the IBM new personal computer (PC) came on the market, the company got its estimates so hopelessly wrong that delivery dates extended over six months and allowed competitors to become established more rapidly than might have otherwise been the case.

Large companies with major investments find it worthwhile to invest substantial sums in developing sophisticated forecasting systems –

General Mills the American food company spent over $1 million in its bakery division – and though such advanced systems are not relevant to the small firm it is important that some form of forecasting system is maintained to identify *change*.

Change is the important feature of forecasting. Are sales continuing to rise at a steady rate or are they starting to decline? How fast will they grow? Or will they decline?

Once a forecasting system is in operation the company will also be able to define the amount of confidence that it can place in it by comparing the actual out-turn of sales in the current year with the previous year's forecast. This will be important for the company in determining the limits within which sales are likely to vary and is crucial to defining upper and lower limits to sales and their effects on other areas of the business.

Developing simple forecasting models

Moving annual totals

The Moving Annual Total (MAT) is one of the simplest and most useful forecasting methods. It provides a month-by-month analysis of what the sales for the previous year(s) have been. It is more accurate than forecasts built on annual sales as it shows trends much more clearly and smooths out the effects of freak sales in any one month or seasonal factors.

The only information that is required is month-by-month sales data over the previous year(s), and this can either be manually maintained or kept using a simple spreadsheet model. The details of how to carry out a MAT analysis are given in the appendix together with the spreadsheet formulae.

MAT analysis does face the drawback that it relies on historic sales data for future sales projection; it is not in other words relating company sales to some factor in the market which may crucially influence the level of sales achieved. Should there be some dramatic change in some factor in the external environment that is directly related to sales any system which relies on historic sales data will be inadequate as a means of forecasting future sales.

Causal models

The other model provided in the appendix can help the small company to define sales trends more accurately as it relies on relating the historic sales to some external factor, which are called *causal models*. For example, the sales of cars have been found to be related to the level of disposable income and the amount of unemployment.

Included in the appendix is the most straightforward causal forecasting method: regression analysis. It allows the manager to correlate external factors with internal sales levels and to ascertain the degree of relationship.

Price trends/inflation

10. Over the past years how closely have the company's products followed the price trends in the market?

Select one of the following, whichever is most appropriate, and enter the answer in the chart at the end of the chapter.

1	2	3	4	5
Very little	Little	More or less	Closely	Very closely

Each industry will have its own price trends which are often different from the underlying national rate of inflation. Electrical goods, for example, have become steadily cheaper in real terms since the 1960s; newspapers, in contrast, have become considerably more expensive.

Input for the business plan

Understanding the price trends in the market place will be central in defining in broad terms the pricing and product policy that the firm will be able to follow. Otherwise there will be two main consequences: the company will become either increasingly uncompetitive and continue to lose market share or increasingly unprofitable.

Seasonality

11. What degree of seasonality is apparent in the industry?

Select one of the following, whichever is most appropriate, and enter the answer in the chart at the end of the chapter.

1	2	3	4	5
Very high	High	Moderate	Low	Nil

Seasonality will have a significant effect on the viability of the business by demanding that high stocks are built up for a particular period of the year with the consequent considerable effect on the company's cash flow. Many small businesses do not realize how dramatic an effect such considerations will have on working capital.

Many of the business failures that occur in the four areas of clothing, drink distribution, building and toys are caused by the effects of seasonality on struggling small firms without the cash reserves to deal with the problems that it causes. Fashion houses sell their collections twice yearly; 60 per cent of house sales occur between April and the end of July; 85 per cent of port is drunk between November and the end of December; 80 per cent of electronic games are bought in the same period.

Input for the business plan

It is crucial that the seasonality of the industry is fully understood – when sales will be achieved together with the timing of payment receipts. For the individual with little experience of a particular industry, the relevant trade association will often have valuable information available to define the likely seasonality pattern.

The firm should also consider reducing the risks caused by a high degree of seasonality by evaluating the range of products sold to see whether the product could be sold in another market as part of an export policy, or additional products can be produced to smooth out the seasonal effects. Examples of such thinking include the Walls Company (sausages and bacon in the winter, ice cream in the summer); and the Jeanneau sailing company in France concentrating on southern hemisphere markets in the winter.

Smaller companies have found similar solutions to problems of seasonality; a firm producing terracotta plant pots (peak sales in the spring and early summer) diversified into kitchen containers; a firm producing wooden mouldings for house interiors (peak sales in the autumn and winter) diversified into producing wooden instead of plastic ends for bathroom light switch cords (produced for £0.15 and selling for £1.00). Readers may, however, like to ponder the problems faced by manufacturers of fireworks and how they might overcome the acute problems of seasonality that they face in the United Kingdom!

Trade fluctuations

12. How high are the long-term fluctuations in the demand for the particular product or service?

Select one of the following, whichever is most appropriate, and enter the answer in the chart at the end of the chapter.

1	2	3	4	5
Very high	High	Moderate	Low	Nil

Trade fluctuations most often occur in the industrial equipment market with machinery being replaced on a two- or three-year cycle. Trade cycles will also be caused by other changes, e.g. increases and decreases in expenditure on roads will be reflected in orders for earth moving equipment. The most extreme fluctuations will obviously be found in the fashion industries.

Input for the business plan

Long-term fluctuations in the industry must be allowed for – by planning for reduced production; developing other areas of activity; increasing promotional expenditure, and so on.

Government aid and assistance

13. Is the company aware of the amount of government aid for the industry or the region in which the business is established?

Select one of the following, whichever is most appropriate, and enter the answer in the chart at the end of the chapter.

1	2	3	4	5
Little idea	Some idea	Fair idea	Good idea	Very clear idea

Firms, like individuals, are extremely bad at exploiting fully all possible subsidies or grants that are available to them. Any rational policy should include the maximum possible use of local and national aid where this is not going to limit future freedom of action. For example, improvements in the surroundings of factory or plant can often be subsidized, but very few companies even approach the local council to find out whether grants are available for such alterations. Similarly the Small Firms Service provides both free literature and limited free counselling on business problems, neither of which are greatly used.

Input for the business plan

All possible grants from both national and local government should be investigated to see whether funding is available for expansion or some specific activity.

Research and development

14. How much money is the company spending on research and development in relation to the competition?

Select one of the following, whichever is most appropriate, and enter the answer in the chart at the end of the chapter.

1	2	3	4	5
30%	50%	65%	75%	90%

For some industries the expenditure on research and development will be vitally important for survival, even for the small company; in others the expenditure will be minimal. For example, small companies producing computer hardware and software will have to spend a very large proportion of their revenues on providing for research and development as otherwise they will be left behind in a fast moving industry.

Input for the business plan

The likely demands of the industry for funds for research and development should be evaluated.

Trade information

15. Is the company aware of how the majority of the customers for its particular product acquire information about changes in the market?

Select one of the following, whichever is most appropriate, and enter the answer in the chart at the end of the chapter.

1	2	3	4	5
Little idea	Some idea	Fair idea	Good idea	Very clear idea

Different industries have differing information sources. Some are very narrow in their sourcing; coverage in one or two journals will suffice or a visit to one or two exhibitions – the vending and toy industries are good examples. Others like education and local government are much more diffuse and difficult to define.

Input for the business plan

Knowing how the industry receives trade information can have an important impact on the allocation of resources. This will be particularly important when the firm attempts to define its promotional requirements.

Planning chart

Enter the answers to the questions in this chapter with a tick on this chart.

	1	2	3	4	5
1					
2					
3					
4					
5					
6					
7					
8					
9					
10					
11					
12					
13					
14					
15					

Marking the respective column and row with the current company position will highlight areas that require additional attention in the business plan: columns 1 and 2 indicate areas of particular concern. The chart provides a ready reference point for later development of the plan, and identifies the most important areas for action. Completing the chart on a regular basis will also enable a comparison to be made year by year of how this aspect of the business has changed.

Summary

This chapter highlights some of the important factors within the industry that the firm should consider.

(a) The exact market that the firm is serving.
(b) Growth or decline within the market sector.
(c) The nature of the competition and how it can affect strategy.
(d) The importance of forecasting future trends.

4 Marketing

Some basic principles of marketing □ Marketing and small business planning □ Distribution □ Product □ Customer dependency □ Sales coverage □ Promotion □ People □ Physical □ Process

By asking some basic questions about the company and the sector it serves in the preceding chapter an attempt was made to arrive at some conclusions about the current state of the business in fairly broad terms by examining it in the context of the industry and market. It therefore seems appropriate at this stage to go one step further, initially by examining some of the basic principles of marketing, and then applying them to the small business.

Some basic principles of marketing

Marketing refers to the understanding that a company must develop about its role in the market, i.e. how the consumer reacts to its product, which consumers buy it, how competition affects the progress of company sales, how the organization should promote itself and its products, and so on.

Segmenting the market

Central to marketing thinking is the idea that the market consists of fairly distinct sub-divisions or segments. Each of these segments have specific product or service requirements. By matching these requirements more closely than the competition the firm can develop market share and profitability.

For the small firm segmentation of the market is a prerequisite to growth and survival; it must strive to find a niche or corner in the market which it can service more effectively than any other.

The marketing mix

Traditionally the important elements that made up the 'marketing mix' were defined as the 4 Ps:

- Price (credit, retail margins);

- Product (quality, product range, packaging);
- Place (where the product is available and how it is distributed);
- Promotion (how the potential consumers should be reached and how the company should push its products).

Over the past twenty years, the steady growth of service based companies (retail outlets, data processing, leisure, food) has emphasized other factors which are equally important.

- People (the involvement of staff will be crucial for most service based companies);
- Process (the way in which the service is provided);
- Physical (the environment in which the service is provided).

A good example of these additional factors in operation is the success of McDonalds. The company spends a large amount of time training its *people*, and has established a central training college or 'Hamburger university'. Its managers keep rigid control over the length of time customers will have to wait to be served, in other words, the *process*. McDonalds also maintain the outlets to a high standard of decor and cleanliness, keeping up the standards of the *physical* environment.

Changing product direction

Companies, whether they operate in the service or industrial sectors, are nevertheless faced with a number of common options when they come to plan for the future.

(a) Abandoning or divesting themselves of products or activities.

(b) Holding the current sales position. This is an essentially short-term option.

(c) Increasing the market share of the product or service in the current market. This may involve:

- decreasing pricing,
- increasing promotion,
- changing distribution methods,
- buying out a competitor,
- branding the product or service.

(d) Selling the product or services in new markets either regionally or nationally. This will involve:

- new distribution systems,
- new salesforce structures.

(e) Changing the products or services for the current markets, which may involve:

- changing current product characteristics – the classic product 'relaunch' of the supermarket: new, smoother, richer, better tasting, easier flowing, etc.;
- expanding the range of products offered to one sector of the market – larger bags of nails for example;
- changing the product to make it suitable for a different sector of the market – producing a gold plated fountain pen for the executive market, for example, instead of steel for the student.

(f) Diversifying the product range in one of a number of ways:

- looking for new products that can be sold to current customers – a firm selling window blinds might, for example, consider that window locks would be a useful addition to the product range;
- identifying profitable products from within the current production expertise – a printer producing books for publishers might see an opportunity to develop in this area on his own account;
- seeing totally new activities which management skills can be applied to – a firm producing bicycles might see major opportunities in running a bus company for example.

Keys to successful product development include:

- distinct product advantage over the competition (an example would be the introduction of Sellotape);
- improved distribution or service arrangements;
- 'image' advantage – often used in fashion industries (for example Nike and Adidas sportswear).

The reasons for failure are more varied but it is possible to identify the more important:

- lack of clear advantage over the competition;
- lack of commitment by people within the company to the new products;
- technical teething problems;
- competitive reaction;
- insufficient investment in the product.

Differences of emphasis

Though companies in all sectors face similar marketing problems there are numerous differences in degree or the extent to which a given factor will be crucial in the marketing mix. The main differences are summarized below and subsequently discussed in the text.

Factor	*Consumer*	*Industrial*	*Service*
Pricing	Crucial	Less	Less
Trial	Less	Crucial	Crucial
Repeat purchase	Crucial	Less	Varies
Distribution	Crucial	Less	Low
Salesforce	Low	Crucial	Varies
People	Low	Varies	Crucial
Packaging	Crucial	Low	Varies
Environment	Low	Low	Crucial
Process	Low	Low	Crucial
Credit	Low	Varies	Varies
Systems	Low	Crucial	Varies

Pricing

Pricing will be a far more important issue for the consumer goods company than companies in the service or industrial sectors where reliability and after-sales back-up are more important.

Trial

Achieving a trial will be far more difficult for the industrial sector company and often for the service company than for the consumer goods firm, as buyers of industrial and service products tend to be more conservative than in the consumer goods sector.

Repeat purchase

Once initial purchase is achieved industrial and service customers tend to be far more resistant to change than consumer goods customers where maintaining a high level of repeat purchase will be important.

Distribution

Achieving a high level of distribution will be more important for the consumer goods company as the majority of industrial based and service based companies will have direct distribution of product from supplier to end user. It will often, however, be a major element of cost in both industrial and consumer product companies.

Salesforce involvement

In the technical areas of the industrial and service sectors a high degree of involvement of the salesforce will be crucial in attaining sales; for the consumer goods company it will often be less important.

People
The involvement and training of people to achieve company objectives will be essential for the majority of service companies, and for some industrial product companies, but far less important for consumer goods companies.

Packaging
Good packaging is often important to success in consumer goods, but less so for the industrial or service company.

Environment
The nature of the environment has a relatively more significant impact on the success of service companies than on industrial and product based organizations.

Process
The way in which a service is carried out is a key feature in determining its acceptability; some industrial based companies with a high service element will face similar constraints.

Credit
Financing the sale of many industrial products by leasing or hire purchase may be an essential part of the sales strategy of the industrial company; credit may be important in many service organizations, particularly retail outlets – turnover in a small department store decreased by 25 per cent when credit was restricted.

Systems
Many industrial and service companies will sell total systems – both hardware and software – for a particular problem that the customer faces. These firms will have to be more flexible than the consumer goods firm that will generally provide a limited range of possible product combinations.

Marketing and small business planning

Like business planning, marketing is often regarded as being of relevance only to large companies. While this may be true of the sophisticated marketing techniques, which are by no means always highly successful in improving overall profitability, some of the basic marketing principles can be extremely valuable in helping the small business to plan its way forward.

Segmentation and the small business

1. How clear an idea does the company have of the functional divisions in the market and the type of product or service that it demands?

Select one of the following, whichever is most appropriate, and enter the answer in the chart at the end of the chapter.

1	2	3	4	5
None	Vague	Some	Fair	Good

Input for the business plan

Central to the formation of a soundly based marketing policy is the ability to define what products may be required by which customers. This can best be achieved by some form of research, however limited and low cost.

Customer research in the small business

2. When was the last time that the company, by way of even a simple questionnaire, sought customers' views on its product?

Select one of the following, whichever is most appropriate, and enter the answer in the chart at the end of the chapter.

1	2	3	4	5
Never	3 years ago	2 years ago	1 year ago	Now

Knowing what customers want and whether the product is totally suitable is crucial for any future development. The information that the majority of companies require is not very sophisticated consisting mainly of the details of:

- product requirements,
- delivery requirements,
- price,
- service level,
- most effective promotional material.

Knowledge of these will often suffice to provide an accurate picture of likely future trends. Employing professional market researchers may give a more accurate picture, but often the results of such surveys lead to the inevitable conclusion that all that is required is more market research. Market research firms, after all, are in business as well!

Input for the business plan

Basic information concerning customers is essential for the future development of the business, and even the most mundane and inexpensive enquiries will often yield valuable results.

The marketing mix and the profit/volume relationship

3. Are the effects on the profitability of the business of lowering and raising price on volume of sales:

Select one of the following, whichever is most appropriate, and enter the answer in the chart at the end of the chapter.

1	2	3	4	5
Unknown	Unclear	Fairly clear	Clear	Very clear

One of the central issues of any business, particularly those that are small, is what the effects of selling more product will be. Many companies associate selling more with improved profitability. *This is not always the case*. Companies need to consider whether the extra sales achieved are:

(a) profitable;
(b) not going to cause cash flow problems (see appendix).

Every product will have two elements of production cost associated with it: costs which are directly related to the production itself (variable or direct costs) and costs which apply to the entire factory or plant (fixed or indirect costs). How these are defined and allocated can make a substantial difference to any one product's profitability, but it is important that the company does define them in some clearly agreed format so that each product can be compared with one another. This approach will also produce a system by which changes in prices and volumes can be integrated into the company's control systems.

A simple profitability model

The factors that any firm has to consider can best be illustrated in an example.

Units		1,000
Price per unit		£50
Revenue (price × units)		£50,000
Variable costs for 1,000 units:		
Labour	5 per unit	£5,000
Materials	10 per unit	£10,000
Discounts	2 per unit	£2,000
Delivery	2 per unit	£2,000
Inventory	1 per unit	£1,000
Total variable cost		£20,000
Fixed costs irrespective of production volume:		
Plant/insurance		£8,000
Sales force		£2,000
Promotional material		£4,000
Total profit		£16,000

Combining these elements on a spreadsheet system, as explained in detail in the appendix, enables the company to:

(a) rapidly evaluate the effects of changing price and other elements of the production cost on profitability;

(b) combine all products to provide a total company picture which can then be integrated with cash flow projections;

(c) allow the company to measure the return on capital employed that each product line generates;

(d) permit the company to calculate the break-even point for each product, i.e. where the product will start to become profitable;

(e) demonstrate clearly the contribution each product is making to overall profitability, allowing for how fixed overheads are allocated;

(f) permit the year-by-year comparison of product performance;

(g) above all it allows the firm to price according to what the market will allow and to see the effects of this upon the overall profitability of the operation.

Far too many firms either add on a margin from the costs of production (cost-plus pricing policies) or set a level of pricing to recover the overhead costs over the year (overhead recovery). Most small businesses miss out badly on the opportunities that exist to price their products more highly.

Profit is the issue. A quotation from Owen Green, the Chairman of British Tyre & Rubber PLC, sums this attitude up: 'Profit is sanity, turnover is vanity.'

Input for the business plan

Evaluating the profitability of each product will be an important factor in deciding on the future objectives and how they can be achieved.

Price/volume relationships

4. How much knowledge does your company have of the effects of lowering price on volume:

Select one of the following, whichever is most appropriate, and enter the answer in the chart at the end of the chapter.

1	2	3	4	5
Very little	Little	Some	Substantial	Very much

Each market will show a different effect of price on total sales. This is termed the price sensitivity or *elasticity* – the percentage drop in sales that each percentage point increase in price relative to the competition will produce. Broadly speaking, there is the greatest price effects with commodities and least with services such as insurance or savings:

Elasticity

High ←——————————————→ Low

Butter —— Pet food —— Cars —— Insurance

For example, butter shows a price elasticity of 10, i.e. a 1 per cent increase in price relative to the competition leads to a 10 per cent drop in volume. Price elasticities in the pet food market are around 5; for the Rolls-Royce motor car probably around 1.2.

Many small businesses do not price correctly and underprice in relation to what the market will pay for a particular product or service. Knowledge of the likely effects of raising and lowering prices will enable the firm to determine the most profitable pricing point for their services.

Calculating price sensitivity

Should the company have access to either detailed or rough figures for the total market sales and the average market price of each product over a two year (or longer) period it will be able to calculate the price sensitivity in the market. Trade associations, trade journals or market research organizations may be able to supply these figures.

First, determine the market average price:

Brand	*Total sales*	*Price*	*Total*
A	1,000	20	20,000
B	2,000	25	50,000
C	3,000	30	90,000
D	3,500	40	140,000
	9,500		300,000

Average price weighted by the volume sold = 300,000/9,500 = 31.5

A similar exercise can be carried out in the following year and the results plotted. Movement in market share related to price will indicate how important price is in determining sales.

Input for the business plan

Analysing past effects of price rises of the company's own and competitive products will give an insight into the price sensitivity operating in the market and how the company should price its products. Forecasting systems can also be used to determine what are the likely future competitive price movements in the market which are a vital part of the pricing process.

Price/quality relationship

5. How does the quality of the company's products compare with competitive products selling at more or less the same price?

Select one of the following, whichever is most appropriate, and enter the answer in the chart at the end of the chapter.

1	2	3	4	5
Very poorly	Poorly	Same	Better	Much better

The quality level that the company achieves will obviously have an important influence on the price that it can command. Research shows that the most profitable solution is to produce products which are of slightly better quality than the competition and sell at a slight premium.

Input for the business plan

Defining product quality in relation to the competition and consumer requirements will be important for long-term development of in-market sales. The best alternative appears to be the production of a superior quality product which can sell at a price slightly higher than the competition.

Discount policy

6. How much of your product range is sold at a significant discount – more than 25 per cent off list price?

Select one of the following, whichever is most appropriate, and enter the answer in the chart at the end of the chapter.

1	2	3	4	5
40%	30%	20%	10%	5%

Discounting destroys profits. Compare two companies selling the same volume of product:

	A	B
Profit at list price	10,000	10,000
Discounted at 10%	5,000	1,000
Discounted at 20%	3,000	2,000
Discounted at 30%	2,000	5,000
Discounted at 40%	—	2,000
Effective profit	8,300	7,200

It is often the simplest solution when meeting sales resistance to offer greater and greater discounts. This will damage cash flow and also tend to weaken any future bargaining position – once the company is known to be 'flexible' on price, future demands will make it impossible to improve the discounting position. Belief in the value of your company's products should be reflected in maintaining and supporting your price levels.

Input for the business plan

Discounting policies should be reviewed and new guidelines established, if the current level of discounting is too high. Clear and unambiguous guidelines should be given to all those selling the company's products or services.

Credit

7. How closely has the firm analysed the potential profitable change in credit policy?

Select one of the following, whichever is most appropriate, and enter the answer in the chart at the end of the chapter.

1	2	3	4	5
Not at all	Little	Some	Closely	Very closely

Changing credit policy may have a significant effect on overall sales – a small store group found that tightening up the amount of credit allowed reduced sales by 25 per cent; a wholesaler, in contrast, found that offering credit on some high margin lines increased turnover by 40 per cent.

Input for the business plan

Extending or contracting credit may have important marketing implications. However, any change that is planned in this area will affect the level of working capital that the firm needs, an extension of credit leading to an increase in working capital requirements.

Distribution

Level of stocks/service

8. How closely has the firm analysed the level of stocks that it needs to maintain to achieve the level of service that it considers necessary in the market place?

Select one of the following, whichever is most appropriate, and enter the answer in the chart at the end of the chapter.

1	2	3	4	5
Not at all	Roughly	Some	Closely	Very closely

The level of stock that the firm needs to maintain will be determined by:

(a) the service level of stockholding;
(b) the amount of space available;
(c) cost of storing stocks;
(d) the economic production quantity;

(e) the shelf life of stocks;
(f) seasonality of demand.

Stock levels will fluctuate as product is sold and new production runs are completed.

The company has to set various parameters:

(a) The level of safety stock required for the market = Number of days stock cover × Average daily demand
(b) The maximum level of stock = Safety stock + Reorder quantity
(c) The economic order quantity = $\sqrt{2PY/IU}$, where:

P = cost of order placement,
Y = annual rate of demand,
I = stock holding cost as a proportion of average stock value,
U = unit cost.

For the small business there are three important factors to be borne in mind.

- The service that it provides may be one of the main competitive weapons at its disposal – companies should very carefully assess the level of safety stock that is required.
- The level of stocks is greatly affected by the distribution method that the firm employs.
- The level of stocks is a central feature of the amount of working capital that the firm requires, and the small business should be trying to reduce it as far as possible.

9. Has the firm considered potential financial and marketing benefits in the way it distributes through the trade?

Select one of the following, whichever is most appropriate, and enter the answer in the chart at the end of the chapter.

1	2	3	4	5
Not at all	Little	Some	Detail	Great detail

Any firm faces two options in reaching its potential customers – it can either deliver to them direct or use an intermediary or intermediaries.

Direct distribution

Direct distribution ensures that the firm maintains the maximum amount of control over the product and its pricing. However, it limits market coverage, and the costs of physical distribution involved can often be very high with small widely separated deliveries.

Indirect distribution

Indirect distribution can be achieved by a variety of methods.

(a) *Wholesalers*. There is an increasing development of specialized wholesalers selling products in restricted areas – for example health food and motor accessories. Selling through wholesalers does mean that the company often loses control over pricing, and the price structure will have to reflect the existence of wholesalers in the distribution system to ensure that customers that are serviced direct are maintained.

(b) *Commission agents*. For consumer products with a high margin the use of commission agents may be an attractive proposition for the small company with restricted selling capability.

(c) *Franchising*. This is a steadily growing trend, especially within the service sector, with Body Shop as a recent success story.

(d) *Dealers*. Appointing dealers in specific areas with exclusive distribution rights can also help the small company to achieve a wider distribution base.

Input for the business plan

Evaluating the benefits of wider distribution policy should be a central part of the business planning process.

10. Has the firm any idea of the costs of current delivery methods and of individual deliveries?

Select one of the following, whichever is most appropriate, and enter the answer in the chart at the end of the chapter.

1	2	3	4	5
None	Little	Some	Good	Very good

Delivery costs will be a combination of the size of the order, the distance to be travelled, and the delivery system used. The most extreme will use air courier systems for small items – the author still remembers with horror a bill for £120 for the despatch of a Stilton cheese to Italy for a public relations event! – to the transport of bulk cargo by boat or barge.

Distribution costs for the majority of businesses make up a substantial part of the selling price. One survey across a range of industries revealed an averaged 19 per cent broken down in the following way:

Administration	2.5
Transport	6.5
Warehousing	3.5
Stock	4.0
Order processing	1.0
Receiving stock	1.5

Such a large element of cost suggests a number of measures should be taken.

- Companies should establish as part of their pricing and distribution policy *minimum* delivery quantities and attempt to stick to them rigidly.
- Companies should attempt to minimize the costs of order processing by maximizing the use of technology and minimizing the amount of paperwork.
- Warehousing activities should be organized to ensure that costs are kept to the minimum.

Distribution analysis

Companies should intermittently carry out an analysis of their distribution policy to ascertain whether profitability can be improved by changing the distribution process.

The analysis should include:

(a) present distribution – frequency of order, size of order, lines per order, overall sales per item;
(b) the nature of demand and its seasonality;
(c) the geographical spread of demand;
(d) the level of service that the company considers is necessary in the market place;
(e) the current costing of transport alternatives;
(f) the current warehouse costs and whether these can be changed by investment in new equipment or layout;
(g) the order processing system and how this could be streamlined.

One of the central questions that small businesses must ask themselves is whether they can justify owning their own distribution fleet rather than using haulage contractors or specialized distribution firms when necessary. Most studies in this area suggest that it is only when the firm needs more than ten vehicles that it is more cost effective to own rather than hire.

11. Has the firm considered alternative distribution methods?

Select one of the following, whichever is most appropriate, and enter the answer in the chart at the end of the chapter.

1	2	3	4	5
Not at all	A little	Some	Fair	In detail

Some companies have found that transferring distribution from road to rail has been highly cost effective. For example Taunton Cider has reported a £250,000 per annum saving. Other firms have found that air freight can be a highly cost effective distribution method.

For each freight system there will be an associated stock holding cost in relation to the transport cost. For example, the firm exporting might consider that the additional stock holding required to service Middle East markets if the area was delivered to by truck was offset by the higher cost of air freight.

Input for the business plan

For some firms involved in the export market alternative distribution methods may be highly cost effective. For the majority of small firms in the UK market it is unlikely that changing distribution methods will be relevant in the business plan.

Product

Product viability

12. How much of the company turnover is produced from products more than ten years old?

Select one of the following, whichever is most appropriate, and enter the answer in the chart at the end of the chapter.

1	2	3	4	5
50%	40%	30%	20%	10%

All successful companies tend to place considerable emphasis on the development of new products in order to replace sales lost from declining products and to grow overall.

There are a variety of methods that are used to define the strengths and weaknesses of products. The first involves dividing the products into categories.

- Today's moneyspinners.
- Tomorrow's moneyspinners.
- Dying products – possibly can be repaired with effort.
- Dying products – hopeless.
- Mistakes or failed experiments.

The main problem with such a division is that it often lacks objectivity – especially when the category of failed experiments is considered.

A second theory is that products pass through a 'life cycle' of introduction, growth, maturity, and decline, and the firm can define its product policy by understanding where on the curve any particular product is and take the appropriate action. The table below shows changes to various aspects of product policy according to where the product has reached in its 'life cycle'.

The product life cycle and product planning

Factor	*Introduction*	*Growth*	*Maturity*	*Decline*
Main action	Expand market	Expand market	Defend share	Maximize profit
Marketing expenditure	High	High	Falling	Low
Strategy	Achieve trial	Repeat purchase	Repeat purchase	Selective
Distribution	Limited	Wide	Wide	Selective
Price	Low	Higher	Highest	Declining
Product range	Basic	Improved	Wide range	Reduced

Graphing the progress of the company's products over time will suggest certain actions that need to be taken when the product reaches a certain stage in its development.

Using the product life cycle concept is, however, open to certain problems. One is that the product may not be following a typical life cycle and this may lead the firm to withdraw support just when it is most needed.

Awareness of the possible broad nature of the product life cycle curve may, however, be a valuable aid to thought about likely future directions. For example, in fashion industries such as toys the sales graph is often very angular, with sales rapidly peaking and equally rapidly declining. This suggests that return on investment will need to be rapid requiring a high initial price, followed by discounting to maintain sales at some reasonable level. Simon, the computer game, was introduced at £32.95 – eight months later it was available at £6.95.

A 'fashion' curve of this nature requires different approaches to the market. For example, it is obviously necessary to price highly in the early stages as the return on the investment will have to be rapid – purchasers of fashion products traditionally do not seek repeat purchases.

Another approach to product planning is to consider the contribution that a particular product makes to the cash flow of the company, and the future prospects that it may provide. Products are divided into four categories.

(a) *Cash generators*. Products that have continued for the last two to three years to generate funds for the rest of the business.

(b) *Possible cash generators*. Products in which money is currently being invested with a good chance that they will supply an income in the future.

(c) *Low cash generators*. Products that have been around for a number of years and which do not appear to be going to provide growth opportunities for the future.

(d) *Products requiring high investment* but are unlikely to repay that high level of investment.

Dividing products into these four categories will allow the company to decide on future directions of investment. Should it:

- withdraw the product from the range?
- continue to use the cash flow from the product for other areas?
- invest the proceeds of the product in maintaining its position in the market?
- use money from elsewhere in the company to invest in the product to generate future profits?

Another product planning option is to look at the longer-term issues that may affect the success or otherwise of the product. Will:

- competition significantly increase?
- pricing come under greater pressure?
- the number of consumers remain stable, increase or decrease?

Such methods will allow the company to identify the products that should be supported and developed, those that should be maintained, and the ones that should be withdrawn. It can also be used to analyse the products within a product range to determine their future.

Options for changes in product range include:

- modifying current product;
- adding different sizes or variants to established products;
- extending the range to suit other market requirements.

Input for the business plan

Analysis of the current performance of the company's products will help define the planning objectives for the future.

New product development

13. What level of control is there over new product development?

Select one of the following, whichever is most appropriate, and enter the answer in the chart at the end of the chapter.

1	2	3	4	5
Very little	Little	Some	A lot	Very much

The development of new products is an expensive and time consuming business which can lead to overall business failure in the small company. Though the success of new products is central to the long-term growth of the company, research shows that only a small percentage are eventually successful.

It is important that any organization plans accurately for new products which may include all the phases described below.

- Initial screening – how well will the product fit with current products/production methods?
- Business development – production testing and full pricing. This phase will include any market research that needs to be carried out.
- Test marketing.
- Full product introduction.

New product development may have serious consequences to the company cash flow and needs to be strictly accounted for to ensure that no problems occur.

Input for the business plan

Product development, its scope and cost need to be carefully planned for and included in the development of the business plan.

Packaging

14. If the company uses packaging, what percentage of its product packaging is more than five years old?

Select one of the following, whichever is most appropriate, and enter the answer in the chart at the end of the chapter.

1	2	3	4	5
80%	50%	40%	30%	20%

Packaging in many industries is an important element in success, and even the well established brands update their packaging slightly over the years to maintain the product's acceptability and the premium price that the company is trying to obtain. Many packaging companies offer free design advisory services.

Input for the business plan

Packaging should be continually reviewed and the costs and benefits of packaging renewal, where necessary, allowed for in the business plan.

Branding

15. How much does the company exploit the branding opportunities that exist in the market?

Select one of the following, whichever is most appropriate, and enter the answer in the chart at the end of the chapter.

1	2	3	4	5
Not at all	Little	Some	A lot	All

Branding the company's products or services where possible has a number of advantages.

- It enables the company to become known more quickly.
- It often allows a higher price to be charged for the goods than might otherwise be possible. Take, for example, running shoes: non-branded product will only command a £8–10 price range, whereas Nike and Adidas for much the same product will be selling for £30–40.

The disadvantage is that the development of a branded goods policy will often demand higher promotional expenditure, and will often exclude the product from a number of distribution channels.

Input for the business plan

The costs and opportunities of branding should be evaluated.

Customer dependency

16. How much do the eight most important customers contribute to profitability?

Select one of the following, whichever is most appropriate, and enter the answer in the chart at the end of the chapter.

1	2	3	4	5
80%	60%	50%	40%	30%

It is inevitable that the company's more important customers will contribute a substantial proportion of sales. Indeed there is a rule of thumb called the eighty/twenty rule which states that normally around 80 per cent of business will be derived from 20 per cent of the customers. When these customers are limited in number, however, the supplier company becomes very vulnerable: the loss of one customer can mean that 20 per cent of sales volume disappears overnight. More important is the effect on profitability – that 20 per cent of sales volume may account for all the profit. In some industries, such as restaurants and the building trade, with a high level of business failure a supplier will have to be particularly aware of this potential problem.

Input for the business plan

An important objective may be to reduce the dependency of the business on one particular company.

Sales coverage

17. What percentage of sales are achieved from outside the company's immediate area (for some firms this will mean nationally, for others outside the city)?

Select one of the following, whichever is most appropriate, and enter the answer in the chart at the end of the chapter.

1	2	3	4	5
2%	10%	15%	20%	30%

A wider sales coverage will reduce customer dependency; it will improve understanding of the market and the competition; it will provide new challenges and stimulation. One survey has showed that small firms only exported around 1 per cent of their turnover, and though large markets such as the USA and Japan are notoriously difficult to penetrate (Acorn Computers is reported to have lost about £10 million in a futile launch in the USA) small scale developments in Western Europe may initially be well worth exploring. Sales expansion will often involve investment in time and money to produce material suitable for new markets – new packaging, administration and distribution costs will all need to be considered.

Input for the business plan

The potential for sales expansion will need to be closely evaluated together with the likely developmental costs.

Sales effectiveness

18. What system has the company for evaluating the effectiveness of the individuals involved in the selling of the company's products?

Select one of the following, whichever is most appropriate, and enter the answer in the chart at the end of the chapter.

1	2	3	4	5
None	Very sketchy	Some	Accurate	Very accurate

Personal selling is a very expensive exercise – current estimates put the overall cost of the average sales representative at around £25,000.

Companies should review the effectiveness of the salesforce in a number of areas.

- How effective is the sales representative in finding prospective customers?
- How many calls per day are made and how effective is the preparation for them?
- How many calls are made for each order, and what return does the company achieve on a day-to-day basis for the investment that it makes in the sales personnel?
- Has the company accurately defined the number of times a company should be visited in relation to the amount of business that can be

generated? It is often valuable to separate customers into a number of categories according to the amount of business that they do with the company, namely:

Category A – to be called on weekly;
Category B – to be called on fortnightly;
Category C – to be called on monthly;
Category D – to be called on quarterly.

- What would be the potential return to the company of recruiting extra personnel for the sales function? How much return would be provided for the extra investment in labour.
- Can a telephone sales system be introduced for repeat orders which would enable the individuals involved in selling to spend their time developing new business rather than taking repeat orders?
- How much selling time is taken up on non-essential paperwork, attending exhibitions, chasing payments and dealing with customer complaints? Many small businesses expect their salesforce to deal with a wide range of non-sales tasks which often considerably decrease their effectiveness.

Promotion

Public relations

19. When was the last time the company contacted the local newspapers or trade journals with news of its activities?

Select one of the following, whichever is most appropriate, and enter the answer in the chart at the end of the chapter.

1	2	3	4	5
Never	5 years ago	3 years ago	1 year ago	Currently

Many companies fail to appreciate the value of regularly contacting trade journals and local newspapers with stories concerning problems or successes. These newspapers and magazines are nearly always chronically short of material and, providing the story is interesting, will print it together with suitable photographs. Such exposure can generate considerable interest within the industry – interest which would be far more difficult to generate by advertisement.

Input for the business plan

The potential of promoting new products and events more efficiently will need to be explored and such items should be included in the promotional budget.

Promotional effectiveness

20. When did the company last evaluate the effectiveness of the promotional expenditure?

Select one of the following, whichever is most appropriate, and enter the answer in the chart at the end of the chapter.

1	2	3	4	5
Never	5 years ago	3 years ago	2 years ago	Last year

Most companies develop a fixed attitude towards promotional expenditure which is often unrelated to its effectiveness. Major consumer goods companies, for example, spend the bulk of their promotional budget on television promotion without, surprisingly, researching the effectiveness of this expenditure, even though it runs into millions of pounds.

Research indicates that the distinction between media or above-the-line expenditure (newspapers, magazines, radio, posters, television) and non-media or below-the-line methods (leaflets, point of sale, catalogues, brochures, exhibitions, trade gifts) tends to be reflected in long- and short-term effects on sales; above-the-line expenditure resulting in long-term sales development and below-the-line in short-term changes.

Whatever the method used, companies can get a fairly accurate measure of the effectiveness of the method utilized. For example, some of the following measures can be used in different circumstances.

- Exhibitions: number of enquiries/cost; value of follow up business/cost.
- Magazines: number of coupon enquiries/cost; value of business/cost.
- Catalogues/leaflets: number of enquiries/cost; amount of business/cost.
- Sampling/merchandising: volume of orders/cost.

Identifying each item of promotional material will enable the company to estimate the most cost effective method of advertisement. This is an important element in calculating the amount of expenditure that should be directed into promotions and the type of material that is most likely to prove effective. Some market sectors will demand a high level of promotional investment – cosmetic firms, for example, will often spend between 20 and 30 per cent of their turnover on promotion – while firms producing steel wire will tend to spend less than half of one per cent.

Input for the business plan

Defining the likely return from various methods of promotion will be necessary to determine:

(a) the total desired expenditure and the likely return on investment,
(b) the most cost-effective media.

Potential consumers gain information about products or services in a number of ways.

(a) *Personal contact:* family, friends and business acquaintances. This would also include the sales representative.

(b) *Pack information:* the product will itself convey valuable information to potential new customers – the pack on the shelf, the new car on the road, for example.

(c) *Editorial comment:* information on the product from 'unbiased' sources such as consumer group magazines, and expert comment in specialist magazines for example.

(d) *Paid promotional activity:* this for many firms will be by far the most important method, but small firms should not ignore the other avenues.

How the firm divides its promotional investment between the various areas will depend on the nature of the product and the market. In some markets – such as the pop music industry – editorial comment is an essential part of the promotional plan; record promoters with contacts in the industry are employed to gain editorial coverage.

For many specialized markets the individual approach of the sales representative may be the most cost effective and/or acceptable in the culture. For example, a large proportion of cars are sold by door-to-door salesmen in Japan, in complete contrast to Western Europe. Marks & Spencer concentrate on pack information as a means of promotion, placing the product in the store with sufficient information on the nature of the product to achieve an acceptable level of consumer purchase.

To spend money effectively in the promotional area will require an understanding of certain issues.

- The promotional requirements of the company and its individual products.
- The agreed level of investment on advertising and promotions by the company.
- The type of promotional material required.

- How to structure the promotional investment during the year.
- How to measure and improve the effectiveness of the advertising.

The functions of promotional material

It is a delusion for any company to consider that promotion by itself will procure success in selling a product or service. The history of new product failures is filled with brands that were launched on that assumption. The old maxim 'you can sell anything – once' ensures that consumers can be manipulated by high promotional expenditures to an extent, but repeat purchase will be extremely limited. The small business cannot in any case afford to experiment with high promotional expenditure to try to attract customers on a 'one off' basis. Promotional expenditure in the small firm must be geared towards securing repeat business.

Different audiences will respond at differing rates to different types of media – some will take in most information via the written word, others will rely more on hearing. Naturally many people do not watch the television, read magazines, listen to the radio, or walk by poster sites. These variations in human behaviour further complicate the task of the advertiser in getting the material to the right person who may be interested in purchasing the product. Furthermore, the messages sent out by most methods will tend to be unequally distributed. For example, the individual glued to the television set may be able to see over 1,000 commercials a week, with a much higher level of repetition for many commercials, than the individual who is working on the night shift.

This has ramifications for the small business even though it will not normally be interested in television advertising. For example, because people often combine visits to cinemas with eating out, local restaurants may find it worthwhile to use local cinema as a promotional medium, especially during holidays and weekends. Since the audience will in all probability have travelled to the cinema by car, local garages often also make similar use of this medium. In this way some of the promotional problems inherent in mass communication techniques can be ironed out to the advantage of the small business.

The content of a company's promotional material, irrespective of its size, will depend on the intended audience, the products and the medium chosen.

Broadly speaking promotional material can perform a number of tasks.

Education – information

It is currently fashionable for a number of agencies to claim that advertising does not seek to influence consumers but to educate and inform them. Semantics apart, it is true that promotional material has a very important role to play in providing potential customers with hard information about the company and its products, particularly if they are new. Especially pertinent to this educational role is written material.

Its form and content will depend upon the company's promotional aim and its audience. Thus a leaflet designed for use in a mail shot will differ radically from a follow-up brochure giving more attention to the merits of particular products. In the first instance the material will be brief, easily understood and will concentrate on the company or product's special features – remember, it may be the secretary, for example, who draws the attention of the boss to a new item of office equipment. In all this the leaflet will be not dissimilar to a radio or television commercial in aiming to stimulate the interest of potential customers.

Follow-up material will be more specifically aimed at supplying the information needs of buyers where this is relevant to the company or product concerned. This will be most important for new products and highly technical items. JCB, the earth moving equipment firm, specialized during its early days in bringing out highly detailed material explaining the merits of their products. BMW in the car market have also concentrated on such an approach and have also been highly successful.

There is also an important role for educative material in re-establishing old products by identifying a new benefit that the product contains. Marmite and Lucozade are two examples, using an educational approach to re-establish an ageing product.

To fulfil adequately the educational and information role promotional material must contain details of important facts, such as location of dealers, full specifications of and modifications to, products. It will be important to make the customers aware of special offers, and forthcoming exhibitions.

Reminders

Promotional material is also used to hold on to current market share by reminding current or previous consumers of the benefits of the product and its continuing presence in the market place. This is sometimes referred to as product visibility. Much of the television advertising and a high proportion of consumer magazine promotional expenditure concentrates in this area. The small company can similarly use ads in the local press and trade journals, or update and re-distribute its promotional leaflets.

Encouragement to purchase

Promotional material can encourage new buyers to try the product. This is especially important when the product is under test or has recently been introduced into the market. Much of sales promotional material will fall into this category and involves techniques similar to those discussed in the previous paragraph.

Aid to product development
Implicit in the earlier discussion is the fact that promotional material can be used to develop new markets and customers.

The responses of customers to a particular type of promotion will vary and will be influenced by a number of factors. It is generally held that media expenditure builds up awareness of the product over a long period of time, eventually causing the consumer to switch brands on a semi-permanent basis. Using sales promotional methods such as 'Buy two get one free', 'The Allied Sale' tends to produce short-term changes in sales but does not appear to generate longer-term alteration in purchasing patterns.

The company in consequence will need to define carefully the timescale over which the promotional material should be evaluated: whether it is seeking short-term sales or longer-term development. The example of Spillers Flour shows the two elements in action. Spillers with the Homepride brand of flour in the 1960s gained considerable market share with their television commercial of the Flour Graders: 'Graded Grains Make Finer Flour'. Budgetary considerations led to the ending of this campaign. To maintain sales against the competition of standard flours and the stoneground/wholemeal varieties that were steadily becoming more popular, the company spent money on short-term promotional activity. In order to combat the growing specialist flour sector the company re-introduced television advertising in 1985 for a new whole-meal variety, using the Flour Graders theme once more.

The different types of advertising material

The main problem relating to promotional material that the majority of small companies must resolve is how to translate promotional requirements into cost-effective management of promotional expenditure.

There are a large number of options before the company wanting to translate a promotional concept into action. Each will have advantages and drawbacks that the company must consider.

A distinction that is made by advertising agencies is to divide promotional expenditure into above-the-line (visible spending via such methods as magazines and TV) and below-the-line (all other promotional methods).

Tables 4.1 and 4.2 summarize the main methods by which customers can be informed about your product or service with their advantages and disadvantages.

Table 4.1 Above-the-line advertising

Technique	*Cost effectiveness*	*Advantages*	*Disadvantages*
TV	100	Widest coverage Maximum control Rapid impact	Expensive Impossible to target accurately Difficult to give technical information Evaluation difficult Difficult to plan
Magazines	75	Easy to target Able to give technical information Can use coupons	Slow build up Reduced impact Difficult to control Hard to show action
Press (national)	65	Wide coverage Rapid build up Easy to plan	Limited impact Difficult to give technical information
Press (local)	80	Easy to plan Poor for giving technical information Relatively cheap	Slow build up Good coverage
Radio	60	Easy to plan Rapid build up Inexpensive	Limited coverage Difficult to show benefits
Cinema	55	Colour and movement	Poor coverage Expensive
Posters	25	Wide coverage Specific target	Expensive Difficult to show benefits Slow to plan

4

Table 4.2. Below-the-line advertising

Technique	*Advantages*	*Disadvantages*
Direct mail	Specific target Can explain benefits	Difficult to control Slow build up Expensive
Exhibitions	Can show benefits Needs careful planning	Expensive Difficult to ensure target group

TV

This is the most appropriate medium for mass market low unit cost products. Average cost of commercial production is around £30,000, with costs of a 30 second national spot at peak viewing time around £18,000. The development of regional TV, cable and other channels does allow the more accurate targeting of campaigns. Channel 4, with much lower costs, has, for example, made it viable for some small businesses to advertise on television.

Magazines

The range of specialist and general magazines enables accurate targeting. Cost of colour artwork for A4 page will be from £200 upwards depending on photography requirements. Costs of insert will vary according to the magazine circulation and the quality of printing, and the size of the advertisement. The use of colour appears to increase the response to an advertisement by about 50 per cent; carefully monitored campaigns have also shown that the response increases as a function of the square root of any increase in size, i.e. doubling the size of the ad will increase response by 40 per cent. Including reply coupons will also improve response but this will vary according to the type of magazine, and there does not appear to be a standard relationship between coupon inclusion and the percentage increase in response, though it is nevertheless always present.

Press

Here again there are wide variations in the level of coverage depending on the type of newspaper: national, local, business or professional. Regional newspapers are most cost-effective for local traders serving general local interests. Artwork costs can be less than £20 for a small block, but circulation will determine the advertising rates. National press is expensive, but good for high levels of coverage. Free newspapers provide a useful service by giving 'blanket' advertising coverage to all homes in an area.

Radio

Production costs are low. Local commercial radio makes it possible to cover specific areas of the country. It is also able to provide rapid build up at low cost – ten seconds on local radio can cost less than £50, but the message will only reach a small percentage of the population.

Cinema

This is an expensive medium limited to one particular type of audience. It is appropriate for certain products but not the majority.

Posters

Posters are expensive to produce and to exhibit but can be specifically directed at one area. They are good for providing information: 'Turn left in ½ mile for Asda'. Widely distributed they supply good coverage for the bulk of the population.

Direct mail

Direct mailing supplies a low cost way of contacting potential clients providing the mailing list is sufficiently specific. The reply rate is likely to be less than one per cent and it is a method which generally needs rapid follow-up by the company with further information. Another method of direct contact is to develop some system of tele-marketing using the telephone to contact directly likely customers.

Exhibitions

Exhibitions can be very expensive. Space at large national exhibitions may be over £300 per square foot and it can be difficult to ensure that the right target audience is attending.

Other promotional material

Leaflets

These are most effective as sources of information to explain product benefits, introduce competitions or special offers.

Firms face a bewildering variety of leaflet formats from folded A4 sheets printed in colour on both sides to single sheet A3 printed in one colour. Complicated artwork, any variation from a standard page format, the use of colour, will all increase the cost. As the level of sophistication increases it becomes more necessary for the firm to produce larger quantities to reduce the overall unit cost. For example, a typical costing for 10,000 leaflets would be as follows:

A4	four colour folded	100
A4	four colour unfolded	90
A4	two colour	60
A4	black and white with perforated coupon	60
A4	black and white	35

Catalogues

These are often essential to provide detailed and full explanations of the features and the benefits of the entire product range. Many firms fail to appreciate the role of good catalogues to aid the establishment of a large product range with the customer. It is quite useful to consider the investment that holiday companies make in brochures to persuade families to book holidays for which, on average, the customer spends around £1,000. Many companies expecting a much greater level of orders from a customer will provide a far inferior catalogue.

Photographs

These are important for public relations activities, for example, coinciding with the launch of a new product or a large-scale exhibition, or the presence of the sales manager at a seminar.

Point-of-sale displays/merchandising material

These are designed for in-store activity to encourage off-shelf movement. They include:

- shelf 'talkers' – promotional material attached to the shelf to draw the attention of the consumer to the product;
- shelf strips;
- mobiles – displays that move in the air, attached to the ceiling near the product, emphasizing one particular product benefit or feature;

- 'dump bins' or special racks for displaying and selling the product.

A specialized form of point-of-sale material is the 'tent' card used in restaurants, cafes and bars to promote particular items available within the outlet. Other specialized material of this nature would include drink mats, ashtrays, and mirrors with product information.

This type of material is increasingly difficult to use in the majority of British retail outlets, as the 'Big Five' (Sainsbury's, Asda, Dee, Argyll, Tesco) do not allow promotional material to be displayed in-store.

On-pack material
This includes all material that is attached to the product in some form or fashion to improve sales.

'Flash' packs are specially printed with promotional material, which may be competitions, self-liquidating offers, money-off offers or additional product. An example would be '30p off next purchase'.

'Banded' packs have material such as free gifts attached to the pack. Twin packs with promotional material is another possibility, the two packs being sold at a special promotional price. The dishwasher packet that includes the rinse aid would be an example.

One survey details customer preferences for special packs:

Extra quantity packs	100
Reduced price offers	92
Free gifts	49
Free mail-ins	42
Self-liquidating offers	38
Games and competitions	32

Both industrial and service companies can usefully explore the on-pack idea, with, for example, software houses including vouchers for discounts off other items of software in the range.

Directories or year books
Ensuring entries in the relevant directories or year books can be an important item in the provision of promotional material.

Audio-visual material
With the advent and worldwide spread of the video, a substantial amount of promotional material is now being provided on video. This is particularly relevant for exhibitions and the promotion of complex and expensive technical equipment.

Trade promotional items
There is a wide range of promotional items produced to provide

4

reminders to trade buyers of the company's products. Examples are key rings, notepads, pens, ties, cufflinks, badges, certificates, wallets, diaries, calendars, executive toys and other desk top items. Often this material is very expensive and of dubious value in achieving any sales objective. The Pirelli calendar became a status symbol, but did it sell any more tyres?

Setting publicity budgets

The amount of money that the company has available to promote each individual product will significantly affect the type of publicity material that can be considered. Most firms do not regard advertising as an *investment*. Promotional expenditure in the small firm can and should be regarded as similar to any other type of expenditure in plant, buildings or personnel, all of which are necessary to achieve profitable sales development.

The majority of firms use one of three common approaches towards promotional expenditure.

Affordable method
This considers advertising as an afterthought within the company planning process, a form of insurance, perhaps. The logic of this approach would be to examine the following figures:

Sales:	£150,000
Variable costs	£60,000
Fixed costs	£60,000
Income:	£30,000
Net profit required	£20,000

and to conclude that therefore the amount of money available to be spent on advertising is £10,000!

The drawbacks of such a method are obvious: the level of promotional expenditure will fluctuate from year to year, often from quarter to quarter. Cynics within the advertising profession notice that marketing managers within large companies often spend a large proportion of their advertising allocation within the early part of the financial year, perhaps to ensure that it is not taken away from them later on!

Percentage of sales method
This considers that advertising should be viewed as being generated by sales: each case sold can provide for a unit of advertising revenue. Though such an approach has accounting advantages by ensuring that advertising

expenditure will not run out of control, it ignores the investment concept of advertising that some products in some markets will produce good returns, whereas expenditure on other products in other markets will be merely wasted effort.

Competitive parity
This is the 'keeping up with the Jones' syndrome. It suggests that the competition knows the industry better (does it?) and that it has the same objectives in every market (does it?). *Promotional expenditure is all about trying to gain competitive advantage* – what is the competitive advantage in doing exactly what the competition does?

An alternative
A more rational approach is to define the investment criteria that the company is using for each particular product. This can be treated as a four stage exercise.

Stage 1: Defining the product needs. There are various planning aids to the definition of promotion requirements, though they need to be treated with caution as they are an *aid* to planning rather than a crutch. The most commonly used is the product life cycle, described earlier in this chapter, which estimates that the promotional requirements for the product will vary as the life cycle proceeds.

These planning methods allow the firm to define which products require additional investment of promotional money to ensure that the maximum return from the products continues to be available to the company.

Stage 2: Defining the level of promotional expenditure. In an ideal world, companies would be aware of the relationship between promotional expenditure and the level of sales achieved. With rare exceptions, this is unfortunately not the case as the majority of companies do not have the time or the money to carry out the long-term testing necessary to define the relationship more clearly.

The most sensible way for the majority of companies is to review past sales performance and how individual products have responded to promotional expenditure, and from that to estimate the likely sales levels at 50 per cent of current, current, and 150 per cent of current promotional expenditure levels, producing some form of analysis of the effectiveness of the promotional budget both within product areas and also promotional categories, in order to maximize the return to the company:

Expenditure level (%)	0	50	100	150
Sales of A	3,500	6,000	7,500	10,000
Gross profit (£)	1,050	1,800	2,250	3,000
Advertising cost (£)	0	500	1,000	1,500
Net profit (£)	1,050	1,300	1,250	1,500

In this particular example the current level of promotional expenditure is far from optimal – either decreasing or increasing the promotional budget would both lead to improvements in profitability. Other analyses on different products would yield different results. What it does define is the likely return on investment of every pound spent in promotion.

The above example would suggest that increasing the level of advertising above the current state of 100 per cent to 150 per cent would provide the best solution rather than reducing it to 50 per cent.

Comparing the return that promoting one particular product will produce in comparison with the other products in the range will determine where the majority of promotional effort should be placed, providing this matches company objectives.

Stage 3: Determining the price/promotional inter-relationship. Once the optimum level of promotional expenditure has been determined the company should consider how price will be affected by the level of promotion. Can the level of advertising support a higher price, improving company profitability? Here some knowledge of the price elasticity or sensitivity of the company's products will be useful.

Taking the figures from the previous example, and comparing sales levels at 10 per cent less or more than the current £1 per unit, might produce the following picture:

	-10%	0	+10%
Sales units	4,200	3,500	2,800
Sales revenue (£)	3,780	3,500	3,080
Costs (£)	2,940	2,450	1,960
Return (£)	840	1,050	1,120

Such a calculation would suggest that the company could raise the price and gain profit even though the volume would decline. Following such calculations at various volume levels one can develop optimum price/promotional interactions.

Stage 4: Advertising in-house or using an advertising agency. Many small firms will find that for the majority of low budget activities (local press, leaflets, catalogues) it will be unnecessary to employ a specialist agency. For more ambitious activities it is probably advisable to consider involving them.

There are three vital steps that should be taken when considering advertising agencies.

(a) They should not be far away geographically, otherwise a large amount of time will be wasted in travel.

(b) The firm should have a *completely clear* advertising brief specifying the product and its characteristics, the target audience, and the desired outcome of the advertising investment.

(c) The firm should *specify* the total investment that is available before the advertising agency begins work and clarify the way in which it will be paid.

People

Standards of service

21. What specific service standards has the company set for employees?

Select one of the following, whichever is most appropriate, and enter the answer in the chart at the end of the chapter.

1	2	3	4	5
None	Few	Some	Many	Very many

For companies operating in the service sector it is essential that both employer and employees have a clear and common idea about the standard of service they are striving to achieve, for example:

- how quickly should customers be served;
- how should complaints be handled;
- what rules exist for payment methods.

One of the lessons of the expansion of franchises is that the franchising company that manages to maintain high standards of service throughout their network will tend to be successful whereas those that ignore this issue will tend to fail.

Input for the business plan

For service companies it is essential that there is a clear understanding of the level of proficiency expected from their employees in close contact with customers. For consumer and industrial companies this may also be important. Training of personnel should be a very important consideration for the marketing mix in the business plan. Training in consequence will have a very important impact on the performance of service organizations.

Performance monitoring

22. What type of system does the company have for monitoring the performance of its operations?

Select one of the following, whichever is most appropriate, and enter the answer in the chart at the end of the chapter.

1	2	3	4	5
None	Occasional	Informal	Formal	Extensive

Monitoring the public image of the company will be crucial for the success of many service organizations, and any company should consider how it can effectively and objectively monitor its own performance. This could perhaps involve getting outsiders to pose as customers and report on their reception.

Input for the business plan

As part of the control process companies should consider how they can integrate a monitoring system into their activities.

Physical

Surroundings

23. What experience has the firm of experimenting with changes in the physical environment to see whether this will improve sales?

Select one of the following, whichever is most appropriate, and enter the answer in the chart at the end of the chapter.

1	2	3	4	5
None	Occasional	Informal	Formal	Extensive

There is a wide body of evidence showing the effects of environmental factors on sales in retail chains and it is likely that many of the same criteria operate in other service operations.

(a) *Lighting*. Many people suffer from slight claustrophobia; reducing this effect with good lighting may improve turnover.

(b) *Heating*. Air conditioning in one West London grocery store increased turnover by 30 per cent during the summer.

(c) *Layout*. Where the most expensive items are kept, how they are displayed, all have an effect on sales.

(d) *Colour*. The use of colour can either stimulate or depress potential purchasers.

(e) *Noise*. Certain studies suggest that the use of music can increase the level of purchase. Carpets on the floor can also reduce the level of noise and make the environment more pleasant.

(f) *Smell*. The introduction of fresh bakeries into stores is thought to increase overall sales of non-bakery products.

Input for the business plan

Companies should continue to review their investment in outlets where there is close contact with the consumer to ensure that maximum sales are being achieved with the current physical environment. Building societies have been especially good at this, and this is partly responsible for their successful acquisition of a greater share of public savings.

Process

Service technology

24. How closely has the company considered the potential for improving the speed of service by technological innovation?

Select one of the following, whichever is most appropriate, and enter the answer in the chart at the end of the chapter.

1	2	3	4	5
Not at all	Some	A little	A lot	In detail

The quality of service provided by the company's employees needs to be backed by the speed and efficiency of the service process.

Increasing efficiency in this area can give the company a considerable edge over the competition. Building societies, for example, have reduced the length of time it takes to withdraw or deposit money by the use of appropriate technology, thus improving the speed of service.

Input for the business plan

Companies should also consider whether investment in speeding the service process would be worthwhile and integrate the costs in the business plan.

Summary

Correct understanding of the marketing environment can be seen as crucial to the success of the firm. This chapter has considered what segments of the market the company should be concentrating on, and what issues need to be considered for pricing, product, promotion and distribution. For the fast growing service sector problems of particular interest such as the involvement of staff, their surroundings and the way the service is performed have also been considered.

Planning chart

Enter the answers to the questions in this chapter with a tick on this chart.

	1	2	3	4	5
1					
2					
3					
4					
5					
6					
7					
8					
9					
10					
11					
12					
13					
14					
15					
16					
17					
18					
19					
20					
21					
22					
23					
24					

Marking the respective column and row with the current company position will highlight areas that require additional attention in the business plan: columns 1 and 2 indicate areas of particular concern. The chart provides a ready reference point for later development of the plan, and identifies the most important areas for action. Completing the chart on a regular basis will also enable a comparison to be made year by year of how this aspect of the business has changed.

5 Production

Costing system □ Production run costs □ Machine utilization □ Levels of components and raw materials □ Range evaluation □ Obsolescent stock □ Quality control □ In-house manufacture □ Sub-contractor dependency □ Packaging and manufacturing efficiency □ Labour productivity □ Machine replacement □ Premises suitability/layout □ Technical assistance

All firms, whether they operate in consumer, industrial or service sectors, face production problems. However, it is not untypical for the service based company to consider that it does not need to analyse the production process. Yet experience shows that it is often in this very area that major savings can in fact be achieved.

In drawing up a business plan the firm must examine its policies in the areas discussed in the remainder of this chapter.

Costing system

1. What percentage of production is accurately costed in terms of direct costs like material, labour, machine time?

Select one of the following, whichever is most appropriate, and enter the answer in the chart at the end of the chapter.

1	2	3	4	5
Nil	10%	40%	70%	90%

Accurate costing is essential to measure profitability correctly so that the company can precisely determine its objectives. Though some companies calculate the overall cost including the contribution to overheads, the marginal production cost is far more important in defining effective profitability (*see* Chapter 3). Many companies, however, do not have the slightest idea of what various items cost to produce; how such companies expect to operate profitably in the long-term is always a mystery.

Example

Steelframe Ltd, a company in North London, was engaged in the construction of shell frames for small commercial developments. They were asked to quote on detailed drawings within two weeks of receipt. As they had not introduced a method of costing, contracts were either extremely profitable or lost money and the company never reached the stage where it could expand beyond the initial ten employees.

Input for the business plan

Accurate costing systems are essential for long-term business survival; their introduction if not currently in operation should be a central part of a business plan. Each product should ideally be listed with:

- raw material content;
- bought in component content;
- machine time required for completion of manufacture;
- packaging and final processing cost.

Control over the costing process can also be improved by the introduction of standard costs: either in respect of the amount of time that is taken to manufacture, or the total cost of the finished article.

From this an *efficiency ratio* (or ER) can be calculated using this formula:

$$\text{Efficiency ratio} = \frac{\text{Standard costing}}{\text{Actual costing}}$$

For example, the standard costing of a particular batch of product might be £2,000, the actual cost £1,800. This would mean that the production line was working more efficiently than forecast (an improvement of 10 per cent). Reviewing this figure will be important for the costing system to ensure that standard unit costs are accurate over time.

It can also be useful to apply one more ratio to the control process. This is the *capacity ratio*, which simply relates the current production to the maximum potential factory production or throughput:

$$\text{Capacity ratio} = \frac{\text{Current throughput}}{\text{Maximum throughput}}$$

This ratio will identify trends in falling production and clearly show areas within the factory that are not paying for themselves and require further management action.

Production run costs

2. What proportion of the total cost of production of the normal production run is made up of the start-up or setting up costs?

Select one of the following, whichever is most appropriate, and enter the answer in the chart at the end of the chapter.

1	2	3	4	5
50%	30%	25%	15%	10%

The longer the production run, the lower the percentage of start-up cost. In some industries such as printing and records the setting-up cost comprises the major element in the final cost, the raw materials for the actual item being relatively insignificant.

Long production runs, however, produce large quantities of stock with consequent effects on cash flow; in a wide product range the time may also not be available to maintain single item manufacture. Reduction in the product range would obviously permit improved production efficiency providing this matches company objectives.

Longer production runs also reduce the variable production cost of each item, as experience is gained in the production process. For example, it costs £6.50 to assemble a TV in Japan compared with around £12.50 in the UK – a reflection of the far higher volumes produced. This is called the 'learning' curve and it is an important element of the continued dominance of mass production companies.

Example

Modex Ltd, a clothing company in the West of London, was approached by a French clothing designer that wanted small quantities of special mohair cloth for haute couture fashion. Though apparently profitable in themselves the orders continually interfered with the standard production runs of cloth for the British market. As set up costs of manufacture were extremely high, the French orders reduced the profitability of the core operation.

Input for the business plan

The implications of longer production runs on stock holding and product range should be assessed to consider whether profitability could be improved. The calculation of the volume necessary to achieve the break-even point will be important in the control process (discussed in Chapter 6).

Machine utilization

3. To what extent is the capacity of the existing machinery or plant fully utilized?

Select one of the following, whichever is most appropriate, and enter the answer in the chart at the end of the chapter.

1	2	3	4	5
30%	40%	50%	70%	90%

Many organizations install expensive equipment which then lies idle for most of the time. In consequence the return on capital employed is poor, particularly when the plant is especially expensive.

Mars, the confectionery firm, considers high rates of machine utlization as crucial to obtaining good return on capital employed and considers that twenty-four hour production seven days a week maximizes this return. Similarly a south coast cinema chain has discovered that the re-introduction of morning screenings for children together with late night speciality shows has greatly improved their financial performance.

Input for the business plan

Maximization of machine utilization should be an important consideration in the development of the business plan.

Levels of components and raw materials

4. When did the company last evaluate the amount of components and raw materials required to maintain production levels?

Select one of the following, whichever is most appropriate, and enter the answer in the chart at the end of the chapter.

1	2	3	4	5
Never	5 years ago	3 years ago	2 years ago	Currently

Raw materials and components cost a considerable sum of money in the majority of companies and are a major part of the individual company's working capital requirements. In consequence, any reduction in stock requirements will improve the company's financial position.

Large companies have been much influenced by Japanese manufacturing techniques that have developed the 'just in time' philosophy whereby raw materials only arrive when and where they are required in the production process and not before. Though such systems are not practical for the typical small business, any manufacturer should ask itself if there are any ways that it can reduce its raw material and component stock holding, by changing suppliers or changing the ordering system.

Example

Claythorn Ltd, a caterer supplying the North Sea oil rigs, continually suffered from the peaks and troughs of demand. By substantially increasing the amount of sub-contract work it was able to cope with the customers' demands without an increase in stock holding or staff.

Input for the business plan

Controlling the level of raw materials will have a substantial impact on the capital requirements of the company.

Range evaluation

5. How frequently does the company evaluate the range of products that it produces in relation to the effects on production efficiency?

Select one of the following, whichever is most appropriate, and enter the answer in the chart at the end of the chapter.

1	2	3	4	5
Never	Rarely	Sometimes	Yearly	Six monthly

The demands of the market will often mean that the range of products that the company manufactures or services that it provides continually expands. Each particular product line will demand its own production run, its own inventory, adding to the working capital requirements of the firm. This often conflicts with the demands for long production runs and consequent economies of scale.

Input for the business plan

Management should from time to time consider whether the current range of items is too extensive for maximum production efficiency.

Obsolescent stock

6. How much of the company's finished goods is more than six months old?

Select one of the following, whichever is most appropriate, and enter the answer in the chart at the end of the chapter.

1	2	3	4	5
25%	20%	15%	10%	5%

Most companies hold in their warehouses cartons of products with the attitude 'we must do something with this'. In many cases this product is several years old: Airfix, the toys and games company, for example, held twenty-two years' stock of certain models produced five years previously! Obsolescent stock ties up cash, space in the warehouse, and lines on the stock sheet. Any company should conduct periodic reviews of the stock levels of slow moving items with a view to keeping stocks as low as possible and generating cash for them. A further factor that should be considered is that as the stock gets older it will become progressively harder to shift it at any price – early action will pay greater dividends than delay.

Example

Chantry Ltd, a firm specializing in the sale of garden furniture and statuary, reported a steady decline in profitability, which led to a cash flow crisis. Analysis of the stock holding revealed that over £200,000 of stock had not sold over the last six months. Removal of the obsolescent stock and concentration on the rapidly selling lines enabled the firm to move into profit within three months.

Input for the business plan

An important objective for the company holding substantial quantities of redundant stock is to dispose of it.

Quality control

7. What system of quality control does the company use for the goods and services that it produces?

Select one of the following, whichever is most appropriate, and enter the answer in the chart at the end of the chapter.

1	2	3	4	5
None	Informal	Some	Intermittent	Rigid sampling and testing

Companies continue to prosper on the quality of their products and services, and it is vital that consistency is maintained. In manufacturing industry this can be achieved by laid-down sampling and testing procedure against performance guidelines. Frequently this will have the added bonus that the amount of wastage within the production process is reduced as major problem areas can be easily identified and corrected.

5

Quality control is also important in reducing the level of working capital. A high level of returned products means less money flowing through the company. Quality control procedures can be further improved by the involvement of the company personnel in the production process.

In the service industries similar performance guidelines as mentioned in Chapter 4 can be introduced for employees. McDonalds, for example, has guidelines on how long it should take to produce a Big Mac, how long the counter staff should maintain 'eye contact' with the customers, and so on. The consistency of the McDonalds empire brought about by such detailed controls has done much to ensure its success. Spot checks by McDonalds supervisory staff ensure that standards are maintained. This method can be used in any service organization enabling the manager to find out what the customer has to suffer (or enjoy).

Another useful measure of quality control is to monitor the level of complaints received. Should these be of an unacceptably high level or show an increasing trend it will provide a further indication of quality control problems.

Example

Phantom Toys produced a range of electronic toys mainly for the Christmas market. For many years it had encountered cash flow problems due to the erratic nature of demand and problems with returned stock, as returns from stores ran at 10 per cent of turnover. The hiring of one additional member of staff entirely responsible for quality control enabled them to reduce working capital requirements by 30 per cent and stock levels by 40 per cent by rigid quality control.

Input for the business plan

Implementation of a system of quality control should be examined when drawing up a business plan, and where one exists whether it can be improved should be considered. Such a system allows the company to set targets for the reduction of rejected product or customer complaints.

In-house manufacture

8. When did the company last evaluate the advantages and disadvantages of reducing or increasing the amount of in-house manufacture?

Select one of the following, whichever is most appropriate, and enter the answer in the chart at the end of the chapter.

1	2	3	4	5
Never	5 years ago	3 years ago	2 years ago	Currently

For many firms it may be extremely inefficient to manufacture product on-site. Producing material outside the factory or plant may be a much more viable proposition. The cost of production of Meccano construction toy sets could, for example, have been halved by the use of outside firms to produce components, and merely assembling the product on site.

Input for the business plan

Evaluating the benefits and drawbacks of external manufacture should be an exercise carried out from time to time as part of the business plan. It may reveal the potential for substantial savings as circumstances change over time.

Sub-contractor dependency

9. On how many suppliers is the company dependent for the bulk of its components?

Select one of the following, whichever is most appropriate, and enter the answer in the chart at the end of the chapter.

1	2	3	4	5
1	4	8	12	15

Dependency on one major supplier presents the same problems as dependency on one major customer. It will lay the company open to problems of quality control, price and availability. Though there is often undoubted convenience in dealing with one supplier, other firms in the market may be able to supply a better product at a more competitive price, and dealing with three or four suppliers for one component area will ensure that continual supply will be maintained. This was one of the lessons that the multinational car companies learnt during periods of industrial unrest in the 1960s. Though there were undoubted economies of scale in single site production of components such as transmission and gearboxes, the problems caused by plant shutdowns far outweighed them. The car manufacturers then moved to a multi-sourcing strategy.

Input for the business plan

Multi-sourcing will often reduce component cost but should certainly ensure production stability, and as such should be part of the business plan.

Packaging and manufacturing efficiency

10. How much of the company's product is produced by the most efficient method?

Select one of the following, whichever is most appropriate, and enter the answer in the chart at the end of the chapter.

1	2	3	4	5
20%	30%	50%	70%	95%

Inefficiency in production may lie in many areas:

- design considerations that prevent the most efficient machinery being used;

5

- lack of investment in suitable machinery;
- unsuitable working practices;
- inability to maximize the use of standard components.

Different companies will experience different problems. Unilever Export produced a range of detergent powders for mainly West African markets in non-standard sizes. Because of this the packs had to be hand filled with a consequent increase in price. Alteration in pack dimensions enabled the same quantities of detergent to be filled on the high speed packing line. Gilbey's Gin was sold in frosted bottles – the frosting process was expensive and also introduced glass particles into the packing line. As glass fragments and machinery do not get on well together the line was frequently halted for repairs. Eventually the company decided to replace the frosted bottle with a more conventional one without any deleterious effects on sales. Meccano failed to invest in volume die-casting equipment and the Dinky toys it produced became steadily more and more uncompetitive in price. Fleet Street is bedevilled by problems of the last category – the technology to improve production exists but not the co-operation of the workforce. Design constraints meant that a specialist motor car manufacturer had to produce a range of components specifically for each type in the range. Slightly re-designing the body shell enabled standard components to replace 80 per cent of the customized material with a substantial increase in productivity and profitability.

Example

Boxer Brewery, a family owned brewery in the east of England, found that the traditional bottled products limited their production to 1,000 gallons a day. The introduction of a bottling line of PET plastic bottles enabled them to meet the growing off-licence demand and increase output to 3,000 gallons a day.

Input for the business plan

Redesigning product or changing machinery may have a significant effect on production efficiency, reduction in material wastage, and profitability.

Labour productivity

11. How much has labour productivity increased over the last year?

Select one of the following, whichever is most appropriate, and enter the answer in the chart at the end of the chapter.

1	2	3	4	5
Nil	1%	2%	3%	4%

Currently labour productivity has been improving at around 3 per cent per annum for British industry as a whole. The skills of employees, their flexibility, the nature of the training that the workforce receives, the type of machinery used, the layout of the factory and its suitability to the production process, the ability of the company to manufacture in long production runs, all will affect the level of productivity that is achieved.

Incentive schemes are often used in an attempt to boost production, but unless they are skilfully designed may often be counter-productive. For example, the Meccano incentive scheme resulted in the workforce concentrating on the easily manufactured flexible plastic sheet rather than on the more demanding metal strips. The result was that at the time the company collapsed there were 750,000 flexible plastic sheets and few if any metal strips.

Input for the business plan

Setting targets for labour productivity will be important in determining overall costs.

Machine replacement

12. By how much would replacing the current machinery improve efficiency?

Select one of the following, whichever is most appropriate, and enter the answer in the chart at the end of the chapter.

1	2	3	4	5
50%	30%	20%	10%	5%

Machine and plant may suffer from demonstrably poor performance in relation to competitive equipment; or they may pose an increasing maintenance problem which substantially decreases the amount of time available for production. In both cases it will be important to consider the costs and benefits of replacing the current machinery.

Most machinery will have a fixed life span measured by the increasing likely repair costs and declining overall efficiency. The suppliers of many items of equipment can often lay down a programme of replacement based on an objective assessment of the likely machine life span. For example, suppose in a fleet of 20 delivery vans 6 will have completed more than 40,000 miles at the introduction of the plan. With the annual mileage running at 20,000 miles and the maximum effective life of a van at 60,000 miles it is inevitable that these 6 vans will have to be replaced during the year. Similar guidelines can be developed for production equipment – so many hours production, or revolutions or whatever. Changes in the level of activity will obviously affect the speed at which these items will need to be replaced and it may be valuable to produce a chart to show trends in machine utilization.

Example

Arlex Lamps, a manufacturer of torches and bicycle lamps, found that their products were becoming increasingly uncompetitive against imports from the Far East. A redesign of the product range and investment in a new plastic injection moulding machine enabled them to reduce costs by 40 per cent.

Input for the business plan

A programme of machinery and plant replacement will have beneficial effects on production efficiency. The costs and benefits of such a programme should be a part of the business plan.

Premises suitability/layout

13. To what extent could production efficiency be improved by better layout or a change in premises?

Select one of the following, whichever is most appropriate, and enter the answer in the chart at the end of the chapter.

1	2	3	4	5
30%	20%	15%	10%	5%

Changing the factory layout or premises can often have a dramatic effect on production cost. Jouvain, a firm in the north of France, found that production efficiencies increased by 40 per cent as a result of improved layout. Other firms have found the same effect, particularly where a complex production process is involved with the movement of components from one area to another.

New premises may offer similar opportunities to improve production. A move by Vickers, to improve armoured vehicle production, is reported to have increased output efficiency by 60 per cent, though some of this was due to installing new machinery.

Such considerations will be very important when the firm is faced with a growth in demand. Can such growth be best met by:

- sub-contracting part of the work;
- increasing machine utilization;
- improving factory layout;
- introducing new machinery;
- moving to a new site;
- improving working practices?

There have been both successes and failures as a result of separating the production process into a number of self-contained units. Howard Machinery, once the largest UK farm equipment manufacturer, failed to ever reach the original levels of production in the five separate sites that was achieved by its single integrated plant. By contrast, the policy of BOCM Silcox to concentrate on small local plants rather than major mills has paid dividends. Beer companies are also moving away from the concentration of brewing on one site.

The lesson that may be learnt from this is that complicated production is best integrated. There may, however, be an argument for dividing production when less complicated products are involved.

Example

Stockholder Ltd, a firm of steel stockholders in the south of England, had continued to grow in their original premises over a thirty year period, with an increasing range of items. In the 1980s they found that they were steadily losing custom, and on investigation it appeared that clients were unwilling to wait the minimum of one hour that it took to fill a large order. Rearranging the way in which the stock was maintained into 'active' areas of rapidly turning stock and areas of less popular items reduced loading time to fifteen minutes on average, and recouped the drop in sales.

Input for the business plan

The effects of improving layouts or moving to new premises should be reviewed annually and the costs and benefits of so doing included in the business plan.

Technical assistance

14. When was the last time the company considered involving outside help to improve production processes?

Select one of the following, whichever is most appropriate, and enter the answer in the chart at the end of the chapter.

1	2	3	4	5
Never	5 years ago	3 years ago	1 year ago	Currently

There are many potential sources of assistance available to solve technical problems. Both the government sponsored technical assistance scheme and support from local technical colleges can provide valuable free advice on technical problems.

Input for the business plan

Free advice – wherever available – should always be explored.

Planning chart

Enter the answers to the questions in this chapter with a tick on this chart.

	1	2	3	4	5
1					
2					
3					
4					
5					
6					
7					
8					
9					
10					
11					
12					
13					
14					

Marking the respective column and row with the current company position will highlight areas that require additional attention in the business plan: columns 1 and 2 indicate areas of particular concern. The chart provides a ready reference point for later development of the plan, and identifies the most important areas for action. Completing the chart on a regular basis will also enable a comparison to be made year by year of how this aspect of the business has changed.

Summary

Cost control within the production process is identified as one of the most important factors that a small business should aim to achieve. From a basic control of costs the business can then go on to evaluate the effects of changing various factors within the production process in an attempt to make the firm more efficient and reduce the working capital requirements.

6 Financial analysis

Accounting systems □ Cash flow □ Overhead control □ Performance ratios □ Bad debts □ Investment analysis □ Tax and pension planning □ VAT and National Insurance payments □ Financing

Successful financial control is crucial to the survival of the small firm. The main issues relevant to the small company are discussed in this chapter.

Accounting systems

1. How easy is it to manage the firm's accounting systems?

Select one of the following, whichever is most appropriate, and enter the answer in the chart at the end of the chapter.

1	2	3	4	5
Not at all easy	Difficult	Fairly easy	Easy	Very easy

A simple, easy to use accounting system should be one of the first priorities of the small business. There are vital reasons why this is so:

- it tells the company where all its money is going;
- it will reduce the accountancy bills;
- it is essential for dealing with queries on VAT;
- it is essential to maintain checks on finances to ensure that malpractice by employees is minimized;
- it provides a mechanism for rapidly identifying debtors;
- it provides the month by month controlling mechanism giving management the information necessary to keep the firm accurately on the planned path.

There are several low cost manual accounting systems available on the market that immediately speed up the accounting process. The author would also recommend that small companies investigate the use of the Amstrad computer and Sage accounting software – more than adequate for the majority of small businesses – with a total package cost of around £750 for computer and software, or Kalamazoo or Simplex systems.

Input for the business plan

Businesses should introduce some form of standard accounting system as soon as possible to gain control over their finances.

Cash flow

2. How accurately does the company analyse and control cash flow?

Select one of the following, whichever is most appropriate, and enter the answer in the chart at the end of the chapter.

1	2	3	4	5
Not at all	A little	Some	Considerably	Totally

Cash flow control is one of the keys to efficient business development and survival. Poor cash flow control is one of the main reasons for business failure.

Even on the basic level businesses should be aware of the movement of cash in and out of the business, when they are occurring, and to what extent cash outflows match cash inflows.

Cash inflow: Sales
Cash outflow: Materials
Labour
Equipment
Rent/rates/taxes
Promotion
Loan interest/dividends

Sales inflow will often be intermittent, as will many of the outflow elements.

How to develop a cash flow model

A cash flow model which will work either manually or on a spreadsheet is given in the appendix. It allows the company to review the effects of raising or lowering prices, discount levels, credit periods, promotional expenditure, the effect of changing interest rates on loan capital and so on.

There are a number of ways that a company can improve cash flow.

- Invoice as soon as possible, and if the contract is a lengthy one ensure that the firm is able to invoice as the work progresses.

- Keep bank accounts down to a minimum if possible; pay money in daily, and transfer any cash balance to deposit accounts so that interest is gained on the money.
- Deal with customer complaints as rapidly as possible so that there is no delay in payment.
- Offer discounts for rapid payment and attempt to reduce credit periods for poor payers or if possible insist on payment on delivery (not often practical for many businesses). Make one individual responsible for the chasing and collection of payment – this is a continual task that requires day-to-day responsibility.
- Investigate the possibility of using factoring agents so that cash is received more rapidly. Experience suggests that factoring needs to be approached *very cautiously* as though the theory is excellent the majority of customers react negatively to the introduction of an intermediary between the supplier and themselves.
- Pay large fixed bills by instalments if possible.
- If the company is operating in a highly volatile market, for example exporting to countries with fluctuating exchange rates, or buying commodities which show large-scale price movements, consider taking forward positions to minimize cash flow problems.
- Re-negotiate credit and discounts from major suppliers annually to try to improve costing and credit terms.
- Use part-time labour and outside consultants to deal with demand peaks.
- Minimize stock holding of raw materials, components and finished goods as discussed in Chapter 5.
- For those companies with a high wage cost, consider making as much of the wage bill as possible performance related.
- Consider the possibilities of leasing rather than buying all items of equipment when they need renewing.
- Continually look for low cost credit from whatever reputable source.

Input for the business plan

Cash flow control is one of the key elements of business planning. The consequences of ignoring it can be disastrous.

Overhead control

3. How have overheads, expressed as a percentage of sales, changed over the last three years?

Select one of the following, whichever is most appropriate, and enter the answer in the chart at the end of the chapter.

1	2	3	4	5
Increased by 10%	Increased by 5%	No change	Decreased by 5%	Decreased by 10%

A steady rise in overheads as a percentage of sales may indicate the need for corrective action in one or more of the areas suggested below.

Wages

There is a tendency in many organizations for the wage bill to increase faster than profitability, often with management leading the way. In small firms it is frequently much easier to link salaries with profitability, either to create a profit-sharing pool with a points system on length of service, or an incremental system by which the firm's progress is reflected in incremental wage payments on a percentage basis which reflect the rise (or fall) in profitability.

Premises

Many firms do not consider how to obtain the maximum utilization of their premises. Should the factory be under-utilized, sub-letting, for example, can be a valuable source of additional income. Portable accommodation can also provide valuable additional space for administration staff without moving into expensive office space.

Heating and lighting

There are increasing savings to be made in defining the methods of heating and lighting more accurately, and introducing proper controls.

Expenses

Company policies about permissible expense levels will vary. As any company grows the level of control over expenses tends to decrease. The company can minimize the problems by issuing company credit cards to minimize cash movements, and by laying down firm guidelines as to the level of acceptable expenditure against which expenses can be judged.

Service levels

As firms grow larger the number of people employed to 'service' other parts of the organization tends to increase. The number of secretaries increases, 'assistants' are appointed, and so on. It is important that the company continually reviews this administrative 'tail'. Evaluating the impact of new technology to increase efficiency may be valuable (this subject is discussed further in Chapter 7).

Input for the business plan

Overhead control is an important element in the financial planning process.

Performance ratios

The most commonly used measures of financial performance in the majority of small firms are total sales and gross profit. These only provide a limited window on the overall rate of company progress. There are others that are worth exploring. These include return on capital employed, sales expense and administration ratios, length of credit given and taken, and stock turnover. These are discussed in the sections immediately following this question.

4. How many measures are used by the company to assess the various elements of its performance?

Select one of the following, whichever is most appropriate, and enter the answer in the chart at the end of the chapter.

1	2	3	4	5
2	3	5	7	9

It is useful to review company performance on an annual basis using a wide range of ratios which, when compared with the previous years' figures, will reveal valuable information about company trends that may require action.

The cash flow model included in the appendix will calculate the ratios given below automatically if a computer is available. If not, the simple formulas provided can be used to calculate the answers manually.

Return on total assets or capital employed

This provides an overview of how the business is progressing. It is a far more useful measure of company progress than sales value as it defines the central objective of most companies – to maximize profitability. The company should ideally aim at achieving a higher return on capital employed over previous years.

Return on capital employed (ROCE) is also a useful measure of comparing short-term investment opportunities – the better the ROCE, the more attractive the investment. Longer-term investments require the use of discounted cash flow methods which can be calculated by the method provided in the appendix.

ROCE is calculated using the following formula:

$$\text{ROCE} = \frac{\text{Net profit before tax and loan interest}}{\text{Total assets}/100}$$

Input for the business plan

The company must set, as part of the business plan, the ROCE target that it is trying to achieve. One method that some successful companies use is to look at the capital base of the company and replace whatever is possible with leased items. Mars, for example, leases all that it can: computers, office equipment, buildings, and transport. Though this will inevitably affect cash flow it does mean a much higher return on capital employed since it reduces the amount of capital that is tied up in the business.

6

Gross profit ratio

This is generally considered to be the profit before the operating and administrative expenses – some companies call it GPAFI (gross profit after factory indirects). It is the measure of mark-up on the goods sold.

$$\text{GPAFI} = \frac{\text{Gross trading profit}}{\text{Sales}/100}$$

Variation in the overall gross profit margin compared with the expected out-turn may indicate that the product mix that the company is selling has altered (always providing that overall sales volumes are still being achieved).

Input for the business plan

Gross profit levels will be affected by pricing, quality, promotion and other factors. The gross profit level achieved will also affect the ROCE ratio.

Net profit

This is a useful yardstick for comparison with the competition – the company should be achieving a better ratio than other firms in the same industry.

$$\text{Net profit} = \frac{\text{Net profit (before tax)}}{\text{Sales}/100}$$

Input for the business plan

Targeting the company against the competition may provide useful guidelines for the creation of objectives.

Sales expense ratio

This analyses the cost of sales in relation to overall sales achieved:

$$\text{SER} = \frac{\text{Sales + Promotional expenditure}}{\text{Sales}/100}$$

Input for the business plan

Sales expense ratios will rise with new product developments or expansion into new markets. Should the ratio be rising, the method of selling and promoting should be re-evaluated.

Administration expense

This is an important ratio in many companies since it will show whether the costs of the management and their expenses are taking an increasing share out of the business.

$$\text{AER} = \frac{\text{Administration expenses}}{\text{Sales}/100}$$

Input for the business plan

Administration expenses should be a steadily decreasing ratio as the company grows. If this is not the case the administrators are starting to take too much out of the company.

Working capital ratio

This will provide a measure of how much working capital is required to support a given level of sales, and will indicate the necessary increase in capital needed to fund a sales expansion.

$$\text{WCR} = \frac{\text{Working capital (Current assets – Current liabilities)}}{\text{Sales/100}}$$

Input for the business plan

Growth in sales will demand an increase in capital, and the working capital will provide a useful indication of what that requirement is likely to be. It will obviously be affected by creditor and debtor levels and how capital base is treated (leasing versus direct purchase), the level of stocks, employee costs, and so on.

Control of working capital is central to the management of the small business – small companies should continually be striving to reduce their working capital requirements.

Stock turnover ratio

6

The faster the stock turn the more efficient the business within the limits of the industry – hypermarkets will turn their stock between twenty and thirty times a year, while it is unlikely that an electrical goods manufacturer will turn over its stock more than five times per annum.

This ratio over time will provide an indication as to the health of the business even though the stock turn ratio has to be considered in relation to the overall service objectives of the company.

$$\text{STR} = \frac{\text{Sales}}{\text{Average stock value}}$$

Input for the business plan

Increasing the stock turn will improve cash flow and the profitability of the business.

Length of credit given

This provides a measure of the number of days' credit your company is giving your customers. It is one of the most acute problems that small businesses face; many government reports have commented on the slowness of payment of large firms in comparison with the small, though little has been done about it.

The small business will have to be *realistic* about the level of credit that its customers will in fact get – it is pointless planning the cash flow on 60 days when the reality is more like 85. The ratio is calculated as follows:

$$LCG = \frac{\text{Debtors}}{\text{Sales}/365}$$

Should the calculated figure be different from the theoretical actual there may be debt collection problems or the initial theoretical figure was inaccurate.

One solution to the problem of poorly paying customers is to use factoring companies which take all the risk of collecting the debts and in return provide the company with a proportion of the face value of the invoices. Generally these firms create problems with the client firm by continually chasing the firm for payment. They will also create the impression that the supplier company is suffering from cash flow problems.

Input for the business plan

Decreasing credit levels will again improve profitability and cash flow.

Length of credit taken

This provides a measure of how long the credit period available to the company is and how rapidly it is paying its bills:

$$LCT = \frac{\text{Creditors}}{\text{Total purchases}/365}$$

Input for the business plan

Attempting to gain extended credit will benefit the business. Many large retail organizations thrive on the fact that while the average length of credit given by them is 3–5 days, the credit taken is 50–60, which coupled with a stock turn of 25 times per annum means that they are using their supplier's money to finance their sales.

Current ratio

This provides a measure of the availability of current assets to meet current liabilities:

$$CR = \frac{\text{Current assets}}{\text{Current liabilities}}$$

Input for the business plan

A decline in the current ratio from year to year will suggest that the business is meeting increasing problems.

Quick or 'acid' ratio

This analyses the ability of the business to pay its way on a day-to-day basis.

$$QR = \frac{\text{Current assets} - (\text{Stock} + \text{Work in progress})}{\text{Current liabilities}}$$

The ratio should be always greater than one. Monitoring of this figure is important in determining whether the company is remaining viable and can continue to trade.

Input for the business plan

The quick or 'acid' ratio is one that should be included in all analyses for companies with cash flow problems to identify likely periods where additional finance is likely to be required.

Debt/equity ratio

This relates the financing of the company to the mixture of loans and other short-term debt to owners' or shareholders' long-term capital. It is otherwise known as gearing.

$$D/ER = \frac{\text{Total loans}}{\text{Equity}}$$

High gearing places severe burdens on cash flow, particularly if interest rates change dramatically. Ratios above 60 per cent are a cause for concern.

Input for the business plan

Ratio analysis is important for the small business in its ability to identify trends that require some form of corrective action.

6

Bad debts

5. How has the level of bad debts changed over the last three years?

Select one of the following, whichever is most appropriate, and enter the answer in the chart at the end of the chapter.

1	2	3	4	5
Increased by 20%	Increased by 10%	Increased by 5%	No change	Decreased by 5%

Bad debts can ruin companies, particularly when they occur on large orders or contracts. Companies should also be aware that VAT is payable on bad debts which effectively taxes the company's bad luck or failure to control the level of bad debt.

Input for the business plan

Companies should attempt to minimize likely bad debts by reviewing customer policy and credit reference procedures.

Investment analysis

6. What sort of formal system(s) does the company use to analyse the likely benefits of investments?

Select one of the following, whichever is most appropriate, and enter the answer in the chart at the end of the chapter.

1	2	3	4	5
None	Little	Some	Considerable	Extensive

The correct allocation of limited resources is an extremely important element in the business plan. Compare the likely cash flows of two projects:

	A	B
Year one	–800	–1,200
Year two	–800	–400

Year three	–800	–1,200
Year four	0	+100
Year five	+600	+800
Year six	+900	+1,100
Year seven	+1,300	+1,600

Which is the best investment?

To answer such questions the company needs a common means of comparing varying investment levels and returns over time. This can be provided by using a discounted cash flow system, which essentially reduces the apparent cost and return from various investment opportunities to a common figure.

A spreadsheet model to develop a discounted cash flow system is provided in the appendix. It analyses the effect of various discount rates upon cash flow. If the two projects above are considered with a discount rate of 10 per cent (the rate at which the value of money in this particular instance is declining):

	A	B
	–727	–1,090
	–660	–330
	–600	–906
	0	68
	372	496
	507	620
	666	820
Total	–502	–322

Neither investment is paying for itself even at a 10 per cent decline in the value of money – higher rates of return would produce an even worse picture. Most businesses would demand that the discount rate should be between 20 and 30 per cent.

Tax and pension planning

7. Is the company's tax and pension planning structured to maximize the return to the company?

Select one of the following, whichever is most appropriate, and enter the answer in the chart at the end of the chapter.

1	2	3	4	5
Not at all	A little	Some	Considerably	Very much

6

Taxation and pension planning can improve both cash flow and help in long-term company financing.

Input for the business plan

Tax planning and pension advice is a complicated field. It is worth investigating for the growing company.

VAT and national insurance payments

8. How often are VAT and national insurance payments delayed to help with cash flow?

Select one of the following, whichever is most appropriate, and enter the answer in the chart at the end of the chapter.

1	2	3	4	5
Always	Often	Sometimes	Rarely	Never

It is tempting for rapidly growing small businesses to use VAT and national insurance payments as an extra source of finance, and a survey indicates that around 15 per cent of small businesses take this course. Changes in legislation on the penalties for late payment may in consequence cause severe cash flow problems.

Input for the business plan

The company's cash flow must not rely on delayed payment of VAT and national insurance, so that changes in regulations will not instigate a cash flow crisis.

Financing

9. Has the company a stated policy on where financing will be received from?

Select one of the following, whichever is most appropriate, and enter the answer in the chart at the end of the chapter.

1	2	3	4	5
No	Vague	Some	Clear	Very clear

Where the small business gets its money for expansion will be a central part of the planning process, especially if the company is rapidly expanding.

First the manager will need to take all steps to generate cash for expansion internally by concentrating on profitable business, reducing working capital requirements, and smoothing short-term capital shortfalls combined with the lowest possible interest rate short-term borrowings.

Once these possibilities have been exhausted the small business manager will have to consider longer-term loan capital and will need to take certain factors into account:

- availability,
- cost,
- flexibility,
- the degree of supervision the lending body will want to exercise.

Each individual small business will be in a different position but in general terms the best long-term solution is to attempt to issue more equity or shares in return for long-term financial requirements, once the obvious sources of finance such as re-mortgaging the family home have been exhausted.

Many small businesses fail to exploit obvious sources of low cost finance. These include:

- members of the family,
- local individuals (accessible through the pages of the local journal),
- outlets such as the Venture Capital Report and small business magazines.

These sources will often be prepared to back more speculative ventures than the banks which will generally demand that the business is backed by double the amount of assets for the level of loan that is being considered, though the Loan Guarantee Scheme has altered the position to a degree.

Input for the business plan

Central to any business development plan should be the attempt to finance as much as possible of the increased capital requirements with long-term capital rather than expensive short-term finance. The latter may also be subject to fluctuations in interest rates which has become a particularly acute problem for businesses over the last ten years. Ideally of course the more money that can be generated by the business for investment the better.

The exploitation of the possibilities of the Loan Guarantee Scheme and

Business Expansion Scheme may be particularly valuable in this area, though firms will need to appreciate the time that raising finance can take.

Planning chart

Enter the answers to the questions in this chapter with a tick on this chart.

	1	2	3	4	5
1					
2					
3					
4					
5					
6					
7					
8					
9					

Marking the respective column and row with the current company position will highlight areas that require additional attention in the business plan: columns 1 and 2 indicate areas of particular concern. The chart provides a ready reference point for later development of the plan, and identifies the most important areas for action. Completing the chart on a regular basis will also enable a comparison to be made year by year of how this aspect of the business has changed.

Summary

The health of the business can be determined by an analysis of its financial position. Understanding the way the company's financial position is built up and managing to control it are essential parts of the business planning process.

7 Personnel analysis

Employee involvement □ Profit sharing □ Defining tasks □ Personnel review requirements □ Continuity of employment □ Recruitment policy □ Training □ Sickness and accident record □ Grievance procedures □ Wage negotiation □ Legal requirements of a company

Many firms create grandiose plans while totally forgetting the fact that the only way that these plans can be implemented is by having the right people available to carry out the various tasks. The 'right' people will also need to know the importance of the labour in which they are involved, and should hopefully be enthusiastic about it. Managers in small companies get a great deal of satisfaction from their achievements; rarely is this feeling shared with other employees.

Various issues concerning personnel that should be considered for the business plan are discussed in this chapter. Many are relatively inexpensive, but if implemented will ensure that the firm is more likely to achieve its goals.

7

Employee involvement

1. To what extent do company employees feel involved in what the firm is doing?

Select one of the following, whichever is most appropriate, and enter the answer in the chart at the end of the chapter.

1	2	3	4	5
Not at all	Hardly	Some	Quite a lot	A lot

Management of all firms appear, intentionally or otherwise, fervently committed to observing continuous and total secrecy about progress or problems in the business. This is known as the mushroom principle: keeping their employees in the dark and occasionally feeding them with rubbish. It may well be that this attitude arises from misconceptions about the nature of management: that keeping employees informed about the state of the company will subvert the authority of management, and that knowledge is power.

There will occasionally be matters where discretion and circumspection have to be observed but the lack of confidence in one's employees, which is always implicit in an unnecessarily secretive organization and which may become explicit in a small firm, may actually decrease efficiency. Not only will it cause needless conflict and suspicion, it may also make it impossible to devolve responsibility effectively because only one or two people at the top have access to the correct information. The fact is that secrecy may be a luxury which only the large organization can afford: it can shelve decisions for months until the top man can give the matter his attention.

Successful companies are often those that involve their employees closely with the business. This may take the approach of developing quality circles, holding company seminars or training sessions or even using the mundane notice board to provide information on company progress. In some firms the holding of company meetings every three months to discuss progress is seen as an additional valuable method of keeping employees informed. One small firm found that by such methods they reduced manpower turnover, then running at 20 per cent per annum, by half.

Input for the business plan

Improving internal company discussion should be seen as an important part of the business plan.

Profit sharing

2. To what extent does the company share the profits amongst its employees?

Select one of the following, whichever is most appropriate, and enter the answer in the chart at the end of the chapter.

1	2	3	4	5
Not at all	A little	Some	Considerable	More than 15%

The development of profit sharing schemes can do much to improve productivity, reduce labour turnover, and reduce disputes.

There are a number of approaches open to the company wanting to increase employee involvement.

- Developing a commission system on suggestions for improved company performance.
- Setting profitability targets for the firm. When these are achieved, an automatic percentage increase in all wages is awarded.
- Introducing a scheme to allow employees to buy shares in the company. For the small business with the majority of control resting in the hands of the founder(s) this is generally not practical, especially as dilution of shares makes future flotation difficult, and dividend policy for the small company will tend to be erratic.

Input for the business plan

Improving the financial involvement of employees within the small business is an important way of maintaining momentum.

Defining tasks

3. To what extent does the company define the nature of each individual job and the lines of responsibility that go with it?

7

Select one of the following, whichever is most appropriate, and enter the answer in the chart at the end of the chapter.

1	2	3	4	5
Not at all	Poorly	Sketchily	Fairly well	Well

Defining the nature of the tasks that the individual is expected to perform greatly helps the organization in several ways.

- It informs the employee of what is expected of him or her.
- It defines the performance levels of the job and the responsibility that it entails.
- It provides a framework for recruitment, appraisal and training.
- It highlights the nature of the contract between employer and employee and will serve as a reference point for any conflict that might arise.

Employers under current legislation are obliged to provide employees with a job description within six weeks of them commencing employment – something that is rarely adhered to. The typical job description will include the position of the individual within the organization, tasks performed and performance standards expected. Should the company think that recruits should be provided with a clear statement of their job in the form of a contract of employment the job description will be an essential first step.

Input for the business plan

It is a useful task to define what is expected of each member of the firm with some form of job description.

Personnel review requirements

4. What structure does the company have to review personnel requirements for the future?

Select one of the following, whichever is most appropriate, and enter the answer in the chart at the end of the chapter.

1	2	3	4	5
None	Little	Some	Fair	Good

The company can only survive and develop with the right people growing with the organization and dealing with a steadily changing working environment. The nature of the company will determine the type of individual required. There is, for example, no point in having postgraduate engineers to run machine tools unless there will be opportunities for them in other areas once they have mastered the initial skills. All that will happen is that they will leave for greener pastures. Similarly it is inappropriate to expect a part-time worker without the appropriate skills to use a computer controlled lathe or negotiate with the bank for an extension of the overdraft.

Calculating current staffing requirements

There are a number of methods for calculating basic staffing requirements.

(a) Factory/shopfloor production staff = Total number of units, multiplied by unit production time, divided by total annual hours available per employee.

For example: 500,000 units × 0.05/1,920 = 13 staff
Labour cost: 13 × basic rate = £78,000

(b) Supervisory staff = Supervisor ratio (Worker/supervisors, e.g. 1 to 6) × Shopfloor staff

For example: 0.16 × 13 = 2.0
Labour cost 2 × Basic rate = £10,000

(c) Admin. staff = Account ratio (staff required to service per account) × Number of accounts

For example: 0.002 × 3,000 = 6
Labour cost: 6 × Basic rate = £30,000

(d) Sales staff = Account ratio (can be generated on sales turnover, account numbers, distance travelled per sales representative) × Number of accounts

For example: 0.002 × 3,000 = 6
Labour cost: 6 × Basic rate + Expenses = £60,000

(e) Sales supervision = Supervision ratio × Sales representatives

For example: 0.16 × 6 = 1
Labour costs: 1 × Basic rate = £12,000

(f) Management = Management ratio (employees per manager) × Total work force

For example: 0.05 × 28 = 1.4
Labour costs: 1 × Basic rate = £15,000

Changes in the work load will be reflected in the level of staffing; this can also be altered by changes in equipment, distribution methods and so on.

Calculating future staffing requirements

From current levels the company can determine the staffing demands for the forthcoming three year period for the various categories and from that define the likely recruitment or training requirements.

For example, the company mentioned earlier might foresee the following development of staffing needs with the required recruitment figures (in brackets) by year taking into account likely staff turnover and retirements.

Year	1	2	3
Shopfloor	13 (2)	15 (5)	25 (10)
Supervisor	2	2 (1)	4 (2)
Admin.	6 (2)	7 (1)	8 (2)
Sales	6 (3)	7 (1)	9 (3)
Sales management	1	1	1
Management	1	2	2

The relevance of appraisal systems

Once the broad requirements of the firm have been assessed it will have to be aware of the current potential of the employees and how long it will take to train individuals to fill the gaps in the organization. This will demand some form of appraisal system.

An appraisal system can vary from a highly formal system with grading scales like those used by major firms such as IBM down to the informal annual review. Whatever the process involved it can be regarded as an important part of the manpower planning process and should define:

- any problems or dissatisfaction that the employee has which might lead him or her to look elsewhere for employment;
- training requirements to improve job performance as well as morale.

For example, one small company unexpectedly found that one of its employees, a middle aged lady who had for some time been in charge of the manual accounting system, was keen to learn to use a computer and to improve typing, accounting, and customer information requirements. Allowed to spend £1,800 on a small computer system she has become a central part of the new office organization. Similarly, another individual considered that he might have potential at gaining new business for the company. Given a trial he has since become the most successful new business generator in the firm. All surveys on job satisfaction indicate that pay is generally a less important factor than recognition of a job well done, and the amount of freedom that the individual has to get a certain task done.

The lesson for most organizations is that they do not *even try* to develop the interests and skills of employees through which the firm might benefit. There is a view, validated by the experience in the illustration given above, that the majority of organizations, small or large, do not need to go outside for important skills. If they first examine the potential of in-house employees they will nearly always find someone willing and able to be trained for a new task.

Once the appraisal stage is complete the company will be clear as to the amount of recruitment that will be necessary to fill likely gaps in the organization – who can be trained within the company to take on more responsibility, and who will have to be brought in from outside.

Input for the business plan

Staff planning will define the costs of future developments and will ensure that resources are available in ample time to meet future personnel requirements.

Continuity of employment

5. How many employees have done *exactly* the same job for the last five years?

Select one of the following, whichever is most appropriate, and enter the answer in the chart at the end of the chapter.

1	2	3	4	5
80%	60%	40%	30%	20%

Routine is bad for all of us; the employee doing the same job for a long time tends to become stale and less productive. Change in job content or nature of the job will ensure that all employees gain valuable experience in new areas of the company and are made to acquire new skills. At the same time there are those who can cope well with routine and where an employee is performing well under such a regime it is much better to consult them before meddling with their jobs. These people are unusual and may be difficult to replace.

Input for the business plan

Companies should look at internal movements within the organization to ensure that individuals retain as far as possible a continuing interest in their job.

Recruitment policy

6. What type of procedure does the company follow in recruitment?

Select one of the following, whichever is most appropriate, and enter the answer in the chart at the end of the chapter.

1	2	3	4	5
None	Little	Some	Detailed	Very detailed

Recruitment is one of the vital elements in building up a strong company personnel base. Many organizations fail to maximize the possibilities open to them of:

- ensuring that the best possible candidates are obtained;
- ensuring that these are evaluated effectively for the company's requirements;
- checking that the potential employees are actually what they claim to be;
- considering whether it might not be more cost effective to replace full-time staff with part-time who will tend to be paid less and certainly reduce the national insurance costs. Many firms with a large seasonal element are increasingly turning to this recruitment method. Savings can, however, also be achieved in other areas of company activity.

Input for the business plan

Evaluating company recruitment procedure will ensure that the investment made in new personnel will yield the maximum return.

Training

7. What percentage of company employees have not received any training over the last two years?

Select one of the following, whichever is most appropriate, and enter the answer in the chart at the end of the chapter.

1	2	3	4	5
95%	75%	50%	40%	30%

All organizations get stale over time; staff and management tend to accept one particular way of carrying out the tasks in front of them. This attitude may become ossified in the view that there is only one way of approaching a particular task. Learning about how other firms cope with the same problems will be an important part of the development of the firm together with the acquisition of particular skills such as word processing, selling, and accounting.

Though there are large numbers of expensive courses run by professional organizations to develop particular skills, there are also a vast range of part-time courses run by local colleges and institutions which should be explored initially.

In the context of new technology it is worth mentioning the very valuable contribution that the business plan operation can make. The procedures described in this book involve the examination of every aspect of the business. As they are worked through it is worth considering the contribution that new technology could make. This will ensure that the consequences of introducing new technology are not disastrous, as many larger firms have found because they failed to recognize its possible knock-on effects in other areas. This is also an issue where staff may have a great deal to contribute if consulted.

Input for the business plan

Training needs and costs should at least be considered, otherwise the company will not operate as effectively as it might.

Sickness and accident record

8. How has the level of absenteeism for illness and the level of accidents changed over the years?

Select one of the following, whichever is most appropriate, and enter the answer in the chart at the end of the chapter.

1	2	3	4	5
Large increase	Increase	Same	Reduction	Large reduction

A bad sickness and accident record is symptomatic of problems within the organization, either with the nature of the work (boredom and apathy for example), or the type of plant and building which the company operates (damp walls, poor heating and ventilation). Employee absence for whatever reason is a waste of the company's resources, leading to a reduction in efficiency. A recent survey suggested that the average level of absenteeism in British industry ran at 5 per cent of the working year, indicating a loss of output per employee of around £1,600 per annum.

Some companies, having identified absenteeism as a major element of waste within the company, have instituted procedures to attempt to reduce it. The most successful method appears to be one in which the absenteeism record of the employee becomes a much more important part of the appraisal system – companies that have developed this concept have seen absenteeism halved.

Input for the business plan

It is in the company's interests to ensure that its employees are as productive as possible, and to define their working conditions with this aim in mind.

Grievance procedures

9. How do the grievance procedures in the company operate?

Select one of the following, whichever is most appropriate, and enter the answer in the chart at the end of the chapter.

1	2	3	4	5
They don't	Poorly	Sometimes OK	Reasonably	Well

Grievance procedures are important for the growing company when the manager ceases to have immediate and close contact with all employees. Disputes will often arise between employee and supervisor where there is right on both sides. It should not be the role of grievance procedures to support automatically the supervisor's point of view – such procedures, as those in the Civil Service, do more harm than good in clearly demonstrating the authoritarian nature of the organization. An impartially functioning grievance procedure will considerably reduce the need for disciplinary action and ensure that all the employment legislation in this area is likely to be complied with, eliminating any possibility of appeal to industrial tribunals which can be lengthy, time-consuming and damaging to staff morale.

Input for the business plan

Grievance procedures should be made to *work*. If the company is considering setting up a grievance procedure, be sure of the determination to make it function fairly. Otherwise, once it is established, it will be difficult to correct the faults or to abolish it altogether.

Wage negotiation

10. How are the wage settlement procedures defined in the company?

Select one of the following, whichever is most appropriate, and enter the answer in the chart at the end of the chapter.

1	2	3	4	5
Not at all	Poorly	Reasonably	OK	Well

However the company manages its negotiation it should be clearly defined. Recently there has been a move towards the development of 'no-strike' agreements with binding arbitration clauses. In many small companies such procedures are unnecessary providing the workforce is aware of how wage settlements will be determined.

Input for the business plan

Laying down clear guidelines on how wage negotiations should be conducted should be seen as an important part of the business plan.

Legal requirements of a company

11. How well does the company understand its legal obligations?

Select one of the following, whichever is most appropriate, and enter the answer in the chart at the end of the chapter.

1	2	3	4	5
Not at all	Some	Little	Well	Very well

Ignorance of the law is no excuse, and failure to understand the implications of some of the legislation may have important consequences for any small business:

- the impact of the time off allowed to female employees at the birth of their children;
- the amount and nature of the insurance that an employer needs to maintain;
- the legal constraints on working conditions including health and safety;
- the length of time that records of various sorts need to be kept;
- the responsibilities of directors to ensure that the company is operating correctly;
- the effects of Statutory Sick Pay (SSP) on the company's employees;
- the amount of information that the company should provide for its shareholders and employees;
- the effects of the Sex and Race Discrimination Acts;
- the effects of the Data Protection Act;
- the effects of consumer credit legislation, safety of goods, or contents legislation.

Any or all of these may have important implications for the company at some stage of its development.

Input for the business plan

A review of legal changes that will affect the business should be seen as part of the business planning process to ensure that no problems are likely to be caused by the legislation.

Planning chart

Enter the answers to the questions in this chapter with a tick on this chart.

	1	2	3	4	5
1					
2					
3					
4					
5					
6					
7					
8					
9					
10					
11					

Marking the respective column and row with the current company position will highlight areas that require additional attention in the business plan: columns 1 and 2 indicate areas of particular concern. The chart provides a ready reference point for later development of the plan, and identifies the most important areas for action. Completing the chart on a regular basis will also enable a comparison to be made year by year of how this aspect of the business has changed.

Summary

Personnel policy is often an area that small businesses ignore because they consider that their employees will continue to work without planning and supervision. All surveys of successful firms show that the opposite is in fact the case: the firm that takes an active interest in developing its employees will in the long run be the most successful.

8 Administration

Management liaison □ Communication systems □ Management information □ Record keeping □ Document and letter production □ Order processing □ Trade associations

The organization of a business will have an important bearing on the type and numbers of employees recruited. This will affect the business plan in terms of cost and the type of service that the company can realistically offer. For example, a company in the drinks and confectionery vending industry could decide to branch out into meals. As the service requirements for meals vending machines are much heavier, the firm would have to ensure that there were not only service engineers available but that they could be rapidly contacted away from the office.

The way in which the firm is organized affects the efficiency with which tasks are carried through and the speed at which the company reacts to external events. Those factors which must be considered are discussed in this chapter.

Management liaison

1. When did management last visit the factory/warehouse?

Select one of the following, whichever is most appropriate, and enter the answer in the chart at the end of the chapter.

1	2	3	4	5
Last year	Three months ago	Two months ago	One month ago	Two weeks ago

There is a tendency in all firms for the management to become isolated, to spend all its time in meetings, and to develop the ivory tower mentality. Good administration is never achieved solely by pen pushing: it requires an understanding of the needs of the organization which can only be fostered through regular contact.

It is surprising how many firms move their offices away from the main production sites to more salubrious locations. This will increasingly isolate the administrators from developing problems which they would be fully aware of if close contact was maintained. Similar difficulties can arise in firms with no formal business progress review procedure where each manager works in his or her own patch without ever meeting to discuss problems in each other's areas. This can make it extremely difficult to identify common failings within the company.

Meetings which start and end on time, work to an agenda, and last not more than forty minutes, have a place in any organization. To achieve this will nevertheless make heavy demands on the manager in charge of the discussion. He or she will have to have the strength of personality to ensure that the agenda has priority and that progress is not impeded by red herrings, however well intentioned.

Communication systems

2. How easily are members of the company kept informed of relevant information?

Select one of the following, whichever is most appropriate, and enter the answer in the chart at the end of the chapter.

1	2	3	4	5
Not at all	A little	Some	Easily	Very easily

Many management texts suggest that information flow within the organization is one of the key factors in business success. In common with involving employees within the company, management needs to ensure that relevant information is made available to all those involved in specific areas.

Input for the business plan

Management should be aware of the need for greater communication within the firm and try to develop systems that encourage the free flow of information.

Management information

3. How much information does the company have available to plan and control future activity?

Select one of the following, whichever is most appropriate, and enter the answer in the chart at the end of the chapter.

1	2	3	4	5
Very little	A little	Some	A lot	Too much

The flow of information in a number of areas will be crucial to the ability of the organization to plan and cope with changing market conditions. In common with the business plan, management information needs to meet certain criteria:

- accuracy,
- simplicity,
- usefulness.

Many management information systems fail to meet these criteria. In large companies the information, though accurate, is often too complex to be useful; small companies suffer from the lack of accurate information on which decisions can be based. Internal information, when properly structured, will be most useful in several areas:

- cash flow information, discussed in Chapter 6;
- profitability and volume achievement, covered in Chapter 4;
- customer account information.

Developing a customer database

Customer account information is a particularly valuable data source which can be used to produce a variety of information. It should cover:

- name and telephone number of main contact;
- address and geographical location of customers;
- size of customer by turnover;
- orders for the previous year(s) broken down by product type;
- discount policy;
- credit terms;
- delivery conditions;
- frequency of sales visit (callage requirements);
- forecast sales for current year by product group.

Recording sales information in this fashion manually can provide a variety of data fairly easily when a small number of customers is involved, but when the account base rises above a certain number it will become essential for the company to automate the retrieval system. Standard commercial databases such as D-Base II provide the facility to analyse and maintain a large number of customer records.

Use of database systems will give the company access to certain information. For example:

- profitability by account;
- effects of changing credit terms;
- progress against forecast;
- strengths and weaknesses of different products with different customer types;
- geographical concentration and sales visit requirements.

This information will help the firm to decide where it should be selling; who it should be selling to; what types of product should be concentrated on; and which customers require remedial action to ensure that sales forecasts are reached.

In addition, a number of commercially available computer packages perform these calculations with others such as:

- credit limit checking;
- integration with accounting systems;
- out-of-stock analysis.

External information will often be expensive and irrelevant to the needs of the company. Two areas can, however, merit further attention.

(a) *General industry information.* Available to all firms is a vast range of magazines and newspapers containing industry news. For the majority of companies it is a total waste of time to attempt to either receive or read all of this material, but many firms go to the opposite extreme and read nothing. For each industry there will be one or two journals that contain the basic industry information. These are worth reading and circulating within the organization as part of the management information system.

(b) *Government information.* There is a wealth of material produced by various government bodies which may be useful in solving specific tasks – for example the British Overseas Trade Board (BOTB) provide material for exporters.

Input for the business plan

Developing a simple information system will help the company to control its activities.

Record keeping

4. How many manual account records are entered per month in both sales and bought ledgers?

Select one of the following, whichever is most appropriate, and enter the answer in the chart at the end of the chapter.

1	2	3	4	5
600	400–599	200–399	100–199	99

As the number of entries increase the strains on a manual book-keeping system will become more acute. For a small business it is straightforward and simple to maintain records of a low number of invoices manually. As numbers increase it becomes steadily more sensible to consider the possibilities of automating the accounting system, providing the process can be integrated easily into the firm's activities.

The speed at which the firm needs to extract and use information from the accounts should be the necessary action standard. Account information may be needed on an immediate basis to answer inquiries, or only needed at the month end for reconciliation. As the number of account transactions rises the need for automation will obviously grow but will be far more acute for the firm requiring on-line information.

Simplicity of operation of any retrieval system should again be the keynote: a paper company with 30 employees bought an integrated computer system costing £1,000 a month which both failed to work and could not be understood by the employees; a replacement system leased at £100 per month worked perfectly. Unless the company is prepared to recruit specialist computer programmers, concentration on generally available hardware and software will provide the most error free entry into the development of computerized accounts.

Input for the business plan

The company should assess the opportunities for introducing computerization for accounting purposes if the workload is increasing.

When considering computerization of this area the company *must* be aware of the major problem areas that will undoubtedly arise.

- All computer companies will tend to push hugely expensive integrated systems that are almost certainly far beyond the company's initial requirements.

- The initial cost hides a considerable hidden element in additional training, computer supplies such as paper, extra screens and other peripherals. Small firms should also make absolutely sure that they can ensure continuity of supply of spare parts and peripherals.
- The timescale for introducing a computer system and making it fully operational often will be over six months – and even then the system will probably be running in tandem with the old manual records.
- The chosen software may not meet the company's exact requirements which can mean that they will need to have software specially written for them – a horrendously expensive undertaking.

The author would suggest some of the following guidelines for the company interested in computerization.

- Be absolutely clear about what the system is required to do – mistakes in this area are very expensive.
- Start with the simplest possible system that allows the company to transfer the data built up to a more complex network when the workload demands it.
- Do not initially strive for complete integration of all information – it is rarely necessary and stand-alone systems are far less likely to go wrong (and indeed be manually replaced).

Document and letter production

5. How many letters and documents of mostly a routine nature are produced manually every day?

Select one of the following, whichever is most appropriate, and enter the answer in the chart at the end of the chapter.

1	2	3	4	5
40	30	20	10	0–9

The word processor opens up great possibilities of improving the efficiency of letter and document production. The normal finding is that writing is speeded up between three and four-fold with the introduction of word processing. It has also led in some companies to all staff using the same equipment to produce correspondence – there are no secretaries whose sole responsibility it is to produce letters and the tea.

Again the firm should consider the action standards necessary for letter and document production as they will affect the way the firm organizes its typing load. Should it be considered necessary that all letters should be answered within 24 hours, training staff to use word processing equipment may be essential, but should the time for reply be four or five days, part-time secretarial assistance will be sufficient. For internal purposes many firms have successfully introduced a handwritten note system further reducing the need for secretarial assistance.

Many firms find that telephone costs are one of the least controllable overheads. It is therefore necessary to consider just how important free access by all staff to outside lines is for the effective performance of all jobs in the organization. For example, order processing and sales support staff crucial to a particular business must have access; indeed for sales staff there may be an argument for installing even more expensive car telephone systems. Staff not requiring continual access to outside lines such as employees working in the despatch department can be denied outside lines without seriously affecting the efficiency of the firm. Installing a pay box for private calls could solve some problems.

Input for the business plan

Introducing word processing into the office will speed document and letter production, particularly if there are large numbers of standard letters or documents produced. The company should review the speed at which documents and letters need to be produced.

Order processing

6. What is the length of time between the order being received by the salesman and it reaching the production point?

Select one of the following, whichever is most appropriate, and enter the answer in the chart at the end of the chapter.

1	2	3	4	5
5 days	4 days	3 days	2 days	1 day

Delays in order processing directly affects cash flow. The faster that the company can convert orders into profitable business and be paid, the more profitable the company will be. In some companies in Germany the sales force now use computers which immediately inform both the accounts department and the production point of orders, minimizing the delay in order transfer.

Input for the business plan

Companies should investigate how procedures can be improved by the use of appropriate paperwork/technology to reduce the length of time between order receipt from the customer and its receipt at the production point.

Trade associations

7. Has the company fully exploited the possibilities of belonging to the relevant trade organization?

Select one of the following, whichever is most appropriate, and enter the answer in the chart at the end of the chapter.

1	2	3	4	5
Not at all	Little	Some	Most	All

Trade associations may offer valuable administrative assistance for many companies with trade marks, patents and common approaches to government departments for particularly acute problems. They may also provide valuable sources of industry-wide training schemes and provide funding for such items as overseas sales visits – around 120 sponsored overseas visits were organized by chambers of commerce and other industry bodies in 1984.

Input for the business plan

The relevant trade association may provide valuable administrative support and could be important for long-term business development.

Planning chart

Enter the answers to the questions in this chapter with a tick on this chart.

	1	2	3	4	5
1					
2					
3					
4					
5					
6					
7					

Marking the respective column and row with the current company position will highlight areas that require additional attention in the business plan: columns 1 and 2 indicate areas of particular concern. The chart provides a ready reference point for later development of the plan, and identifies the most important areas for action. Completing the chart on a regular basis will also enable a comparison to be made year by year of how this aspect of the business has changed.

Summary

Administrative efficiency, though less glamorous than sales or advertising, is no less essential for a profitable company.

9 Setting objectives

Defining the business purpose □ Setting relative goals and objectives □ Noting key assumptions □ Defining absolute goals

Once the past history of the company's operations have been analysed, the planner can then move forward in the business planning process by defining:

(a) the business purpose;
(b) relative objectives over the planning horizon;
(c) defining absolute objectives;
(d) providing the detailed numbers that relate to the business purpose and the broad objectives.

It is easier when completing something as complex as a business plan to break its development down into a number of discrete steps. This allows the managers to see exactly where decisions interact. It is often far too easy to shoot forward from analysing past history to completing the business plan by adding 10 per cent to last year's totals.

The value in a step-by-step build-up approach is not to encourage masochism amongst the planning team; it is instead designed to make them *think* about what they are trying to achieve and how they are trying to achieve it.

Defining the business purpose

The first step must be to define, or re-define, the purpose of the business. This should include a brief statement about:

- why the company is in the market;
- what the company does;
- the company's market and financial goals.

An example for a company acting as a distributor of motor car spares might be along these lines:

(a) 'The company operates in the service sector of the economy aiming to satisfy the demand for rapid availability of all spare parts generated by vehicle service and repair centres.' This identifies the fact that the company is not necessarily limited to the car market: its mission is to provide a *comprehensive and speedy delivery service.*

(b) 'The company currently is regionally based and concentrates on the supply of spare parts to major garages which act as distributors and service centres for the top ten motor car manufacturers.'

(c) 'The company aims to continue to concentrate in the area of the market in which it is established; the directors do not see that major growth in the scope of activities is advisable.'

Setting relative goals and objectives

The analysis of the current status of the industry, marketing, production, finance, personnel and administration policies will all yield areas of weakness or problems that need to be tackled.

The issues that are raised by such an analysis will need to be resolved or improved over the planning horizon of the company. As these objectives are fairly broad, it is best to consider these first before attempting to set specific targets. By the time these have been completed and discussed within the company the levels of specific achievement that are possible in years one, two and three will be seen in relation to all the other factors within the company.

Setting relative objectives – an example

A company might find that quality control was a major problem as it analysed its current performance. It might develop an objective to reduce the level of returned goods to 2 per cent at the end of the three year period from the current 9 per cent in this fashion:

Year 1	Year 2	Year 3
7%	4%	2%

Naturally such an objective would have important consequences within other areas of the company operation. This is most usefully defined as *linkage* – the other areas of the company operation affected by changes in one area.

In this example the changes in the level of returned product would affect a number of areas to a greater or less extent.

(a) *Working capital.* Reduced returns would decrease the amount of working capital that the firm needs as the level of stocks held would be lowered.

(b) *Debtor period.* Reducing the level of returns would also tend to improve the speed at which debts were paid.

(c) *Pricing.* The improvement in quality might also improve the overall level of pricing that the firm was able to receive in the market.

(d) *Personnel.* This could be part of an overall profit-sharing scheme. It may also involve the company in a training programme to improve the understanding of the production process, and briefing the salesforce, if one exists, on the new quality control systems that are in operation.

(e) *Labour turnover.* Introducing quality control systems may reduce labour turnover which would have the effect of *reducing* the amount of money that the company is spending on training.

(f) *Administration.* The reduced number of returned products might cut down the amount of time spent dealing with queries.

The next stage in the process would therefore be to note down the linkage items next to the proposed changes:

Factor	*Current*	*Yr 1*	*Linkage*	*Yr 2*	*Linkage*
Quality control	9%	7%	Working capital Debtor period Pricing Personnel Labour turnover Administration	4%	Working capital Debtor period Pricing Personnel Labour turnover Administration

In this particular example the linkage will not change in years two and three, but for many other elements in the business plan there will be additional factors that will need to be considered in following years. Each business plan will differ slightly in the inter-relation of one factor to another but taking time over this particular stage in the build-up of the plan will have certain advantages.

- It will highlight the important building blocks for future success.
- It will further develop an understanding of the business and how each decision that is made will have important consequences in other areas.

For each factor that is linked to the action that the firm considers necessary there will either be a *benefit* or a *cost*. These should also be estimated alongside, either positive or negative.

9

Linkage	*Cost/benefit*
Working capital	Reduced by x
Debtor period	Reduced by y days
Pricing	Improved by z%
Personnel	Profit scheme and training cost for Yr 1
Administration	Workload reduced by b hours week

Related to each of these costs or benefits will be *assumptions* about how these factors are derived.

In this example the company might consider that the following assumptions were important:

Factor	*Assumption*
Working capital	None
Debtor period	None
Pricing	Competition remains largely unchanged Promotional expenditure not decreased
Personnel	Providing no union problems
Labour turnover	Providing wage rates competitive
Administration	Providing customer base stays same

Some of these assumptions will be far more important than others. It is suggested that these are highlighted in the business plan development as they are important when determining how sensitive the final figures are to alterations in the underlying assumptions. Entering key assumptions in capitals will make the definition of the most crucial assumptions much easier, both for the authors of the plan and for other members of the management team who need to know which factors are considered most important by the planners.

Follow this procedure for each of the areas of the business that the company has reviewed from Chapters 3 to 8. First, enter the factors relating to the analysis of the industry in which the company operates. It is probably advisable to find as large a sheet of paper as possible to carry out this exercise (or to enter the findings on a wall chart).

Industry

Factor	*Yr 1*	*Linkage*	*Cost/ benefit*	*Assumptions*	*Yr 2*	*Linkage*	*Cost/ benefit*	*Assumptions*
1								
2								
3								
4								
5								
•								
•								
•								

Now enter the marketing, financial, administration, personnel and production factors in a similar fashion:

Marketing

Factor	*Yr 1*	*Linkage*	*Cost/ benefit*	*Assumptions*	*Yr 2*	*Linkage*	*Cost/ benefit*	*Assumptions*
1								
2								
3								
4								
5								
•								
•								
•								

Noting key assumptions

Remove the key assumptions from the planning charts and note them under their respective headings:

- Industry
- Marketing
- Production
- Finance
- Personnel
- Administration

Defining absolute goals

The analysis of current strengths and weaknesses will allow the company to gain a clearer view of what is attainable. Once these have been discussed, the company will be able to develop absolute objectives which quantify the relative objectives that were initially discussed.

Sales levels will depend on the accuracy of forecasting techniques. The way in which these models can be used is discussed in the appendix, and the development of accurate forecasts of volume should be considered in relation to this analysis.

Absolute goals should consist of two or more key points within the various sectors of the business which are seen as crucial to the success of the business. These should be laid out over a three year period.

An example of absolute goals might be as follows:

Industry
- To develop 10 per cent of total sales in a new industrial sector by year three.

Marketing
- To introduce one new product by year two and a further one by year three.
- To expand distribution by gaining 300 new accounts reducing the reliance on the five major customers to below 50 per cent of total sales.
- To increase the sales volume from 2,100 to 4,800 by year three.

Production
- To introduce new machinery to cope with the raised production.
- To totally replace all current machines by year three.
- To be installed in new open-plan premises by year three.

Finance

- To increase the return on capital employed from 15 to 22 per cent by year three.
- To improve profit margins from 5 per cent to 7.5 per cent by the end of year three.

Personnel

- To reduce the level of labour turnover from 22 per cent per annum to 12 per cent by year three.
- To introduce profit sharing for all employees by year three.

Administration

- To reduce the number of staff in the administrative area from 15 to 12 by year three.
- To reduce the average time taken to process orders from 48 to 24 hours by year three.

These objectives act as the measure of success or failure of the numbers that are introduced into the business plan – does the actual outcome of the business plan match the numbers involved?

These absolute objectives will be used at the end of the planning procedure as a measure of how successful the plan is: how closely it matches all of these objectives.

10 The plan in detail

The planning pro forma □ Sales and marketing □ Production and purchasing □ Personnel □ Administration □ Resource allocation

If the procedures outlined in earlier chapters have been followed the company's broad goals and its business activities should be fairly clear. From this vantage point it is possible to set about preparing a detailed plan for the small business, including the financial forecasts over the planning period, which will relate back to the absolute objectives set by the organization. At this stage, especially in situations where several employees are involved in drawing up and finalizing the plan, it makes good sense to draw up a timetable or control schedule along the following lines:

Area	*Responsible*	*Target Completion*
Sales forecast		
Production forecast		
Labour plan		
Purchasing plan		
Financial projections		

A timetable such as this outlining the tasks, responsibilities and targets will ensure that the aims of the planning exercise remain clear. If a muddle or bottleneck is occurring it will help to identify it, and the setting of a completion date will act as a source of motivation.

The planning pro forma

The final forecasts, budgets and projections for the business plan can be set out in any desired format. As the planning exercise is being undertaken for the benefit of the company the plan should be tailored to the needs of the individuals running it. Thus the formats adopted do not necessarily have to be consistent with each other: the sales forecast, for example, is unlikely to have the same format as the capital expenditure projection. It is, however, crucial, whatever the method selected for presenting the final forecasts, that the approach to preparing each forecast is similar. This will be ensured by working systematically through the various facets of the company considered in the earlier chapters and preparing a series of charts to identify the current state of the business. These will be used as the basis of a *planning pro forma* prepared for each forecast and designed so that, as it is completed for each component of the forecast, one is led logically through the development and calculation of that item.

The company will have already set objectives – the next step is to quantify the plan and ensure that it meets its objectives. *This is a central part of any planning process*: objectives, once set, should be used to review the effectiveness of the plan with the aim that the plan will only be finalized when as many or as much of the objectives can be achieved with the resources available.

Quantification

The planning pro forma is the working paper for preparing the detailed plans, and should be used as such. On it, set out the factors and the basis for calculation used in the computation of each item in the forecasts. Completing the forms will lead to the detailed forecasts and projections, and identify the actions necessary to achieve the forecasts. A separate form should be used in the preparation of each individual forecast.

Where to start

Although in practice many of the individual detailed plans will be prepared concurrently with one another, it is still necessary to find a starting point or one phase of the plan from which the other plans evolve and with which they must be consistent and compatible. This starting point must relate to the business's key objectives. Often it is the sales and marketing plan that assumes the initial dominant role because the key objectives frequently relate to desired sales targets. It therefore makes sense to attempt first to formulate the sales plan and then tailor the other plans to it.

There are nevertheless situations where the sales plan is not of critical importance: cash flow considerations, or the elimination of losses may be the key factors. It could also happen that selling itself is not the problem since the business is able to sell as much as it can produce. In such a case, the manufacturing or purchasing areas may be the key factors controlling the future of the business and become the critical aspects of the overall plan. These situations should, however, be clear in the objectives or goals that have been formulated for the company. If there are doubts about where to start the plan:

(a) refer back to the company's key objectives, and if necessary:
(b) refer back to the charts on the current state of the business.

Timescale

Each individual company will have a different approach to the timescale of the plan, with some planners considering a five year forecast as providing the necessary continuity. Experience suggests that too long a planning horizon just leads to meaningless calculations or 'number crunching'. For all practical purposes a one year detailed projection together with two additional years in outline will provide any small company with a clear indication of future direction. The forthcoming year becomes, so to speak, a 'window' in the development of the firm – two previous years' history, the current year in detail, and then two years' forecast in outline.

Approach to the plan

Here in brief is an example of how one might work through the plan. The overall plan will be divided into sections, each giving detailed attention to key areas of the business such as:

- Sales and marketing
- Production and purchasing
- Product development
- Facilities, plant and equipment, capital expenditure
- Organization, personnel and administration.

When each segment has been examined they will be combined to produce the overall financial forecast, which will in turn lead to the calculation of the company's financial requirements. A vital technique is to prepare the forecast *from several different directions*. For example, when analysing likely sales levels it is valuable to consider by independent assessment what the likely volume by customers will be and compare the figure arrived at with the projected sales on a product line basis, and sales on an area basis. Approaching the forecast in this fashion will ensure that the chances of major error are minimized.

The following sections detail some of the factors that must be considered in preparing the detailed forecasts.

Sales and marketing

Assuming that the sales forecast is considered the dominant theme of the plan, the use of forecasting techniques and the forecasting models provided in the appendix will be extremely valuable in the development of these forward plans. The company needs to consider also at this stage the forecasts for *future years*, apart from the detailed analysis of the forthcoming twelve months. What is the company planning to do in years two and three and how does action in the current year affect what will happen in the future?

In addition to the use of forecasting techniques the use of internal information on the customers that the company is currently selling to will be valuable for planning purposes. Information can be derived as to the nature of the customers, the prices that the company is able to achieve, the level of discounts prevailing, the amount of credit provided and which products or product types sell in each sector.

Examples of the items from which the detailed forecast can be developed will include items such as sales via major customers, sales by customer type and so on. It is useful to include how the calculation is arrived at and also a column which indicates the effect on the cash flow of the firm. Sales to individual customers or total product lines will naturally bring revenue into the firm; some factors will be neutral – for example, maintaining current machinery will not require substantial investment. Many aspects of the firm's activities will involve cash outflows such as wages and new product development. Arriving at estimates of benefits and costs of each proposed action will help in defining those areas of the plan that require major resource allocation, both in the short- and medium-term over the planning horizon.

Subdivision of plan

Item	*Basis for calculation*	*Benefit/ cost Yr 1/ Yr 2*
1. *Volume*		
Major customers	Volume by customer	
Other customers	Total volume	
Possible new customers	Total volume	
Customer type (e.g. restaurants, cafes)	Volume by customer type	
Possible new customer type	Volume by customer type	
Demand by area	Volume by area	
Demand by new area	Volume by area	
Individual products or product lines	Volume by item	
New product or product lines	Volume by item	

2. *Price*	
Major customers	Price obtainable from them
Other customers	Price obtainable from them
etc.	
3. *Discounts*	
Major customers	Level of discount
etc.	
4. *Credit terms*	
Major customers	% 30, 60, 90 day credit
etc.	
5. *Promotional expenditure*	
Major customers	Expenditure by major customer
etc.	
6. *Distribution costs*	
Major customers	Per unit distribution costs
etc.	
7. *Selling costs*	
Major customers	Costs by major customer/unit
etc.	
8. *Research costs*	

Completion of these estimates will allow the company to make decisions about the distribution and marketing methods being used, and other related overheads, together with estimates of the required resources necessary such as:

- number of distribution/warehouse personnel required;
- number and type of delivery vehicles required;
- outside storage/distribution facilities needed;
- number of salesmen/distributors required.

Once these estimates have been made the figures can be provisionally entered in the spreadsheet pricing and volume model provided in the appendix.

Production and purchasing

Once the preliminary sales targets have been developed, attention should then be given to the production and supply side. Matching production with sales will always be a difficult problem but it is essential to the small business to try to control it, since being unable to fulfil orders on time or building up excessively high stocks can be both expensive and damaging.

Starting with the sales forecasts, the first step is to determine the quantities of products that have to be produced or assembled in each period and then to determine what this means in terms of raw materials or components that have to be brought in.

Subdivision of plan

Item	*Basis for calculation*	*Benefit/ cost Yr 1/ Yr 2*
1. Component cost	Volume	
2. Labour content	Standard production time	
3. Inventory cost	Stock cover required	
4. Storage space	Stock cover required	
5. Purchasing/warehouse staff	Volume	
6. Machine requirement	Volume	
7. Maintenance staff	Age/machinery utilization	
8. Space requirement	Machinery utilization	
9. Fixed overheads	Space	
10. New product development	Development time	
11. Training costs	Manpower levels	

Once these costs have been arrived at on a product by product basis they can be entered into the costing model.

New products

If the broad objectives of the business, as reflected in the preliminary detailed sales forecast, indicate the need for or intention to produce a new product or range, then a preliminary plan for its development must be sketched out as it will otherwise interfere with the level of facilities that are available for the production of the current product range. The main factors that should be considered are:

- Who will be involved?
- How long will it take before production can commence?

- What testing will the product require?
- What costs will be involved?

Critical path analysis

The company should introduce some form of method of analysing and controlling the development of projects to ensure that the production occurs on time and hopefully meets the targeted expenditure levels. The most useful technique in this respect is termed *critical path analysis* and involves the linking of events to determine which must occur on time for the project to meet deadlines.

The first step is to list all the various stages in the production process, and the length of time that each of them takes, e.g.:

Receiving packaging material from printers – 3 weeks

The next is to connect the items that are related to each other, e.g. the printer must be provided with artwork on the packaging material before he can produce the packaging material.

Working through the list of items in this fashion will yield the critical path of events that must be followed to ensure that the project meets the necessary deadlines. The analysis of project deadlines in this fashion creates one of the management control tools most useful for the small business which will be critical for future progress. The use of wall charts with coloured strips identifying when activities have to occur and how they are inter-related are valuable visual control methods for the small business.

Further aspects of the plan

For the purchasing and production plans certain other questions are also involved:

- To what extent is it possible to make production more efficient by modernizing plant or processes?
- Could more economical increased production be achieved through subcontracting than increasing in-house capacity?
- When will additional capacity be required? At what point will a decision be needed?
- If expanded facilities are required, can the present facilities be extended or will an entirely new location be required?
- Closely linked to the production plans is the assessment of whether the business premises are suitable, and that there is and will continue to be sufficient plant and equipment to satisfy the production volumes anticipated in the most efficient and cost-effective manner possible.

All aspects of the business's capital assets should be examined. Obvious areas include:

- land and buildings;
- production machinery and equipment;
- vehicles;
- office and data processing equipment;
- furniture, fixtures and fittings.

In the initial assessment and business analysis, the present condition and adequacy of the existing assets will have been reviewed and assessed. In a business that is in operation, the main aim of this section of the plan will be to determine the likely needs in terms of expansion and to plan an orderly programme for the replacement or modernization of the plant and equipment if necessary. For example:

- At one extreme, it may be apparent that the business should move to a new location, possibly due to inadequate room for expansion, or because of a poor present location in relation to markets, raw material and component supplies, transport, skilled labour force, or whatever.
- On the other hand, it may be that the existing facilities are much larger than actually required and are therefore underutilized. It may be possible to dispose of such surplus facilities and use the funds acquired more profitably within the business.
- Two factors must be examined where production plant and equipment is concerned – *capacity* and *efficiency*. Capacity to handle present and planned volumes is obviously essential. It may also be that the present production facilities are old-fashioned and new technology has resulted in the availability of more efficient processing. Although conversion to more modern equipment may involve a large investment of funds that are not currently available, it may be necessary to plan for the introduction of such equipment during the period covered by the plan, because of the longer-term cost savings and benefits.
- A planned replacement programme for vehicles should include all the business's vehicles: the forklift trucks used at the warehouse, the delivery vans, the salesmen's cars, the manager's cars.

The preparation of detailed cost and cash flow estimates for such expenditures will in many instances be extremely difficult. For example, the cost and cash flows will be heavily dependent on the method of financing – purchase, leasing, hire purchase. The method chosen for each particular asset will depend not only on cash availability but also on other factors such as the tax implications of transactions.

In many cases, only broad estimates of the amount and timing of the capital expenditures can be made. The precise costs and timing will often only be determined after a detailed study and evaluation of the acquisition in question. For example, the purchase of a minicomputer system will not normally be undertaken without a study of precise needs and evaluation of a number of alternative systems on the market.

For the purposes of the business plan, however, decisions should be made as to what capital expenditures may be desirable and required, and broad estimates of costs and completion timetables should be set. The actual implementation of these projects will form part of the actions necessary to achieve the overall aims of the business plan.

Personnel

It was stressed earlier that for a business plan to be successful it must be realistic and take into account the resources that are, or likely to be, available. The most valuable resource a small business has is its people. It is, therefore, vitally important to evaluate critically the abilities and experience of the present staff and workforce and also assess the type and quality of people it will be possible to recruit in the future.

For the purposes of the run-through of the plan it will be necessary to translate the preliminary sales and production forecasts into estimated staffing requirements. At this stage, the prime objective is two-fold:

- to estimate total salary and wage costs and related overhead;
- to determine a preliminary recruitment plan in terms of the number and level of people that will need to be hired – or fired – and at approximately what times.

To calculate these figures, a logical analysis of the requirements of each department or operating area will be needed. Again, the use of the planning pro forma will help in ensuring that staffing requirements are properly related and compatible with the sales, production and other targets.

The personnel plan should follow the organization of your business.

Item	*Basis for calculation*	*Benefit/ cost Yr 1/ Yr 2*
1. Senior management	Numbers × Wages	
2. Secretarial/Administrative assistance	Numbers × Wages	
3. Sales	Numbers × Wages + Commission	
4. Production		
5. Warehouse/Stock control		

6. Distribution/Delivery
7. Accounting, sales orders processing and invoicing
8. Recruitment costs

For each it is necessary to estimate:

- the number of staff required in each period covered by the plan;
- their required level of skill/experience/qualification; and
- their approximate cost.

While for an existing business one must inevitably start with the existing staffing and structure, thought should be given to the most efficient and effective way of organizing them, and how this will relate to the objectives that have been laid down earlier in the analysis of the company. Here the company will also need to consider any overall company profit-sharing scheme.

Administration

It is easy to overlook the need to plan for the administrative support systems that will be required. They include:

- operations: order processing, invoicing, stock recording;
- record keeping: accounting and reporting systems;
- secretarial: filing, photocopying, stationery, typing.

The office equipment plan can contain more than at first sight might be expected. Office equipment covers the whole range from typewriters, wordprocessors, photocopiers, telexes and other telecommunication equipment as well as computers. These are used now not only for accounting but also for a variety of operational systems such as order processing, stock control, production control and the generation of a wide spectrum of management information reports.

The requirements for administrative support systems should be evaluated and the planned capabilities of the system always kept in line with the expected volume of business. The implementation and development of the support systems should be regarded as an integral part of the overall plan.

Item	*Basis for calculation*	*Benefit/ cost Yr 1/ Yr 2*
Secretarial supplies	Last year	
Telephone costs	Last year	
Photocopying	Last year	

Resource allocation

Once the initial plans and projections have been prepared for each segment of the business, the overall financial forecasts can be assembled. This is an area where it is valuable to have had an interaction of the planning team. Sales and marketing should ideally initially provide information on sales and volume expectations on a line-by-line basis to the production and administrative planners for them to arrive at the costs of the planned activity separately. The total package of sales, production, and administrative pro formas can then be given to the finance department for further analysis.

These financial projections should consist of:

- cash flow forecasts on a month by month basis;
- profit and loss assessments also on a month by month basis;
- balance sheet calculations on an annual basis.

Illustrations of how these forecasts can all be inter-related are included in the model provided in the appendix. The most valuable exercise for planning purposes is to compare the progress of the business in the forecast year with what happened over the previous two years. Their precise formats can be varied and tailored to the specific requirements and characteristics of the business.

The financial projections will provide an indication of two main factors:

(a) The basic profitability inherent in the forecasts.

(b) The way in which the company will have to consider going about getting finance – when and how much will be required?

The projections will also inevitably produce areas that will need reassessment. These might be as follows:

- The costs of launching the proposed new product are far too high and mean that the company's resources are stretched beyond what is possible.
- Discounts and credit levels are far too high and need to be changed.
- Wage levels are far too high.
- Sales per employee have reduced from previous years, indicating that the business is becoming over-staffed.
- Some products show steadily reducing profitability; perhaps resources should be more effectively channelled into the newer range of items.
- New machinery is too expensive; the firm can only afford one of the three machines that are proposed to be purchased. What effect does that have on the production proposals.

Each department of a business will generally have some good idea of how to spend money. The planning team would be advised to separate expenditure into a number of sub-headings:

(a) Items the business knows how to use and are indispensable to its future progress.
(b) Items that while not indispensable will make the business more profitable and pay back the investment within a fairly limited time.
(c) Items which may help the company but can only be quantified with difficulty.
(d) Items that cannot be justified on commercial grounds but will help staff morale, physical environment of the firm, or some other criteria.

An example might be the provision of a very expensive computer system. Should the firm be highly profitable such an item could be considered under subheading (c); but otherwise the firm would need to continue with the manual system or buy a less expensive system.

In preparing these financial forecasts, a number of areas relating to financial management policies and strategies will have to be examined, reviewed and developed. A few examples might be:

- financing through debt or equity capital;
- income reinvestment as opposed to dividend payout;
- management of cash flows;
- any weaknesses identified during the business analysis, e.g. poor control over collection of accounts, inadequate working capital levels, excess levels of stocks, poor use of surplus assets and funds;
- the purchasing or leasing of new plant and equipment;
- identifying the optimum sources and methods of financing increases in working capital and fixed assets.

When all these considerations have been blended into the overall financial forecasts, the result will be a list of financial projects, plans or objectives to be achieved in order to meet the overall aims of the plan. These financial plans will be just the same as the marketing or production plans. They will involve specific people being responsible for achieving the completion of certain tasks or objectives within a specified time span. Examples might be:

- to identify and obtain necessary sources of funds;
- to improve the system of control over cash collections;
- to complete the evaluation of a lease or buy decision re an acquisition of some new equipment.

11 Finalizing the plan

Cross checking and sensitivity analysis □ Management control from the business plan □ Preparing the plan for outside funding □ Conclusion

Cross checking and sensitivity analysis

Once the main elements of the plan have been finalized the company will be in a position to move forward to review the plan under a number of headings.

Reviewing assumptions

The key assumptions will be central to any checking of the plan that is undertaken. It is worth the entire planning team reviewing the key assumptions and considering what is the likely worst case, and the opposite – what is the best case. Both variations will have significant effects on the business plan.

For example, a key assumption might be on the number of accounts that the company will hold during the year:

Factor	Worst case	Current case	Best case
No accounts	500	850	1,100

The number of accounts will affect many elements of the business plan. It might influence:

- total sales
- discount structure
- distribution costs
- promotion costs
- sales force costs
- administration overheads and equipment

Running through the key assumptions will identify those that are absolutely central to the successful completion of the forecast. It may be, for example, that a reduction in the number of customers by 10 per cent may be far less important than an increase in the amount of credit that the company allows customers or a 5 per cent drop in the gross margin across the entire range of products. Management will be able to identify by these means the two or three *essential factors* for success and to devise a method to monitor the achievement of these levels on a week by week or month by month basis.

Contingency planning

In addition to these limited central factors considering other assumptions will also be a valuable management exercise in that the company can at least think about the action that it will need to take should either the best case or worst case situations arise.

One useful technique is to produce a chart of actions that will need to be taken if the outcome either is significantly better or worse than the forecast:

	Pricing	*Distribution*	*Credit*	*Promotion*	*Product development*	*etc.*
Better						
Worse						

These actions become one of the useful elements of the management plan – they become part of the planning process allowing management to think about what they would do to cope with massive failure or, just as important, how they would cash in on instant success. Contingency planning of this nature is a major help to the small business. As earlier chapters have stressed the manpower resources of the small business will always be overstretched and in a crisis there is normally little time to hold meetings to discuss the problem, and even less time to search around for the solution to a problem that may have become extremely pressing. The partial solution of the problem before it occurs during the planning process will significantly speed up the response of the business to violent changes in the business environment and make it better able to cope – the ability to keep your head while all about you others are losing theirs may be the sole difference between survival and extinction.

Reviewing the effects of changing the assumptions on the outcome of the business plan will lead onto the next element of finalizing the business plan, comparing the forecast year with previous history.

The evolving business – comparing forecast with past history

Assumptions are most easily tested against the experience of previous years. Does the forecast appear to be soundly based on what has happened in the previous two years? Key comparisons that the company should make include:

- Is the projected pricing in line with what has been achievable in the market?
- Is the volume attainable on the customer base that is proposed?
- Is the level of credit and discounting largely consistent with previous experience?
- Does the level of material, labour, selling and administrative costs reflect what has previously occurred?
- Has the company accurately reflected the timescale involved in any new development, e.g. the time for installing and commissioning new equipment or the training of new staff, in the projected plan when compared with similar experiences in the past?
- Has the cash flow projection taken into account the experience the company has had previously in raising money and especially the payment of intermittent sums such as VAT, rent and rates, national insurance?

Particularly valuable in this respect will be the comparison of the ratios that are part of the cash flow model provided in the appendix.

- What trends are shown by the comparison of the ratios over the two past years and the forecast period?
- Does the return on capital employed fall over the three years or does it fluctuate alarmingly?
- What changes can be seen in the gross profit ratio, either increase or decrease, and is it a cause for concern?
- Are sales and administrative expense ratios increasing or, as they should be, showing a steady decline?
- The working capital ratio trend will also reveal whether the company is tying up more money in production and stock or increasing credit unnecessarily.
- Does the creditor and debtor ratios indicate that corrective action will need to be considered?
- Is the company likely to experience increasing financing problems shown by the debt to equity ratio, and quick ratio?
- Are sales and profits per employee increasing or declining?

The future business - considering implications of forecast for future

The cash flow model outlined in the appendix allows the company to consider the effects of future growth on the funding requirements of the business in the following two years and how the ratios are changing. The company is then able to see a five year spread of progress:

–2 yr	Last year	Forecast year	Yr + 1	Yr + 2

Such a format enables it to maintain consistency in the planning process and also allows it to maintain progress towards the achievement of the main business objectives.

Assembling the detailed plan

The model in the appendix is designed to provide the framework within which the progress of the business can be monitored. Following a series of logical steps such as those below will allow the planner to build up the numbers on a month-by-month basis.

1. *Defining the total sales value.* The most likely level of total sales will be the first item to enter derived from the marginal profitability analysis spreadsheet.
2. *Examining seasonal trends.* These will be available from past records or, for the new company, industry data will provide some form of indication of likely seasonal pattern.
3. *Total monthly sales.* Total sales considered with the seasonal pattern will yield the month-by-month sales pattern.
4. *Credit terms.* The business will have set objectives on the level of credit that is given.
5. *Monthly cash flow.* This will then be derived from total monthly sales and the credit structure.
6. *Additional income.* The company will be able to enter additional income that will arise as the result of the business plan.
7. *Production/selling costs.* These can be entered from the marginal profitability model as a percentage of the planned production level (increasing or decreasing volume will inevitably affect this figure which will need to be updated on a regular basis).
8. *Administrative costs.* These can be derived from the analysis in Chapter 10 as a percentage of the planned level of sales.
9. *Additional costs.* These will be derived from additional investment

requirements in replacing machinery and other equipment and planned levels of expenditure on rent and rates.

The model will then calculate from these key items of information and others on which the business has to decide (depreciation levels, for example) the cash flow and profit and loss statement for the forthcoming year.

Consistency with objectives

Defining the detailed figures is often so time-consuming that the planners miss one of the most important aspects of the planning process: the consistency of the plan with the original objectives that the company has set. In other words, how does the plan meet the initial objectives that the company had laid down? Rarely will a plan match all the objectives exactly, but does it over the three year period achieve as many of the objectives as possible?

As a final part of the planning process the company should review the detailed plan that it has developed within this framework, i.e. the level of achievement that the plan allows over the period considered:

Objectives	*Level of achievement*
Marketing	.
Finance	.
Production	.
Personnel	.
Administration	.

Management control from the business plan

The business plan, as has been stressed, is a working document. It is not designed to be filed away in some drawer and forgotten, but rather to be used as a measure of management control against which the company can monitor actual levels of achievement.

If possible every business should try to hold a monthly meeting away from telephones and interruptions:

- To discuss the achievement of the month's action plan: what has been achieved and what problems need to be overcome?
- To review quickly the key assumptions on which the plan is based – have they significantly changed and what effect will this have on the business?
- To monitor actual sales levels achieved and, most important, the level

of gross profit – what implications does this have for the planned level of turnover and profitability? or production levels? stock holding?

- To review the cash flow projection. Is the company achieving the level of cash flow forecast in the business plan?

These control measures conducted on a monthly basis will ensure that the company keeps a close watch on all aspects of the business that are most likely to cause failure: cash flow, profitability, and the failure to meet deadlines on the development of new projects. In addition, on a quarterly basis, a more detailed investigation of the profit and loss account will be a further valuable control method.

Preparing the plan for outside funding

Though the plan is a document which is most useful internally to make the business work more profitably and efficiently, the majority of occasions that a small business will formally complete and collate a plan will be when some external finance is required for future development. For the majority of firms this will involve contact with the local bank, or private individuals/companies interested in small company investment. A smaller percentage may contact venture capital firms.

Central to any consideration of the proposal is the need for the funding institution to be SURE that the plan is workable and that investing in the proposal has a high level of likely return. The key issues will be:

- *S* – is the business *soundly based*. Is it likely to meet a long-term demand in the market?
- *U* – does the business *understand* what it is doing?
- *R* – is the plan *realistic*? All plans by their nature tend to be optimistic, but does the plan stretch the limits of credibility?
- *E* – are the members of the company sufficiently *experienced* to carry out the demands of the operation? Do they have the necessary skills and expertise for the new enterprise?

The business plan prepared for outside bodies will therefore have to take these factors into account and highlight the crucial factors and problems that the plan addresses.

Contents

I. *Summary*. Not more than one page which defines the problem, the solution, and the action necessary.

II. *Table of contents*.

III. *Business purpose*. This should clearly define the nature of the business and where the company is attempting to reach during the period of the plan.

IV. *Key objectives*. What is the company trying to achieve over the plan period regarding:

1. *Marketing*. What are the key objectives: volume, distribution, competitive position, pricing?
2. *Financial*. What are the main financial objectives: level of profit, return on capital employed, cash flow?
3. *Production*. What are the key production objectives: productivity, plant design and layout?
4. *Personnel*. What are the main personnel/administration objectives?

V. *Market summary*. This should contain the analysis of market, market trends, customer base, market share within relevant market sectors over the past three years, comment on major competitors, and how the company is more effective than others in the market.

VI. *Marketing plan*. How the company plans to take advantage of its market opportunities broken down in whichever way is most appropriate, for example market sectors, or customer types. The plan should comment in detail on: product, price, distribution methods, promotional techniques that will be used, people, physical aspects, processes involved.

VII. *Production availability*. How the company organizes its production: how dependent it is on outside suppliers for components; how efficient the machinery is for the sector of the market which is being serviced.

VIII. *Organization and personnel*. An organization chart should be included with numbers, what type of negotiating structure exists and whether there are any profit sharing or share ownership schemes in operation.

IX. *Senior management*. The plan should include in substantial detail the experience of all the senior management team for the task in hand. This is often a major failing of many business plans: a key factor in most funding exercises will be the level of expertise in the company to cope with the demands of the proposed project.

X. *Financial forecasts*. The company should show clearly:

1. The financial history of the firm with a five year trading history if possible.
2. Details of current forecasts concentrating on ROCE, cash flow, gross profit and other key ratios.

3. Details of the financing required, how much is needed with the terms required together with the proposed re-payment schedule.

Conclusion

Where have you got to?

Efficient application of the principles of planning provides the firm with a competitive advantage. In other words, it is able to use its resources more effectively than other firms to be more profitable and grow more rapidly. The business plan is going to help the small business by answering these questions:

(a) *What can the firm achieve?* Producing an integrated view of the entire market, which allows the development of an effective long-term strategy.

(b) *Where are the greatest opportunities?* Defines medium-term investment criteria from the long-term strategy to invest in new products or services.

(c) *How can the firm take advantage of them?* Helps the firm to decide where it should position both new and old products to achieve the best result consistent with the long-term strategy.

How does it help you?

In the words of John Townsend, writer of *Up the Organisation* (Pan 1975), one of the most entertaining books on organizations:

'If you're not in business for fun or profit what are you doing there?'

On an individual level the planner should develop a clear view of what the organization should be trying to achieve, this year, next year and into the future, and, most importantly, should find it:

Fun
Stimulating
Satisfying

12 Case studies in small business

Introduction

The case studies that are included in this chapter serve to highlight certain of the issues that have been raised in Chapters 1–8. How should companies go about developing their businesses? Have they taken the right or wrong decisions? What marketing, financial, production, and administrative issues will be important for them to solve so that they can achieve profitable business development?

The small business

For the small business interested in developing an effective plan which will impress an outside funding organization, it is most valuable to look at these case studies as a bank manager would. Does the business as it is portrayed inspire confidence? What questions should the managers of that business be asked in order to come to a decision about whether or not to provide funding. Approaching the case studies in this fashion will provide the small business with valuable insight into their own plan. Does it exhibit any of the same worrying features that have been identified here?

The student

For the student the case studies provide an opportunity to develop skills in the analysis of business problems. Though there is no hard and fast way of approaching a case study as they often differ considerably in length and complexity, the following guide has been found by the author to be functional and effective for a whole range of material.

1. Initially read the case quickly to gain an overall impression of what the key factors are likely to be.
2. Identify and analyse what data will help in defining the problem.
3. Complete the analysis by carrying out a SWOT (Strengths, Weaknesses, Opportunities and Threats) analysis.
4. Determine the possible paths of action, and their implications short-, medium- and long-term.
5. Define the constraints under which the business is operating.
6. Decide on the best solution for the problems facing the business and compare it with the solution proposed (if any) in the case.

Case 1: Turner Power Tools

Cyril Turner, a former Sales Manager with Brent Power Tools Ltd, decided in 1983 to set up his own business, Turner Power Tools, situated not far from his previous employer. He began his work supported only by administrative help from a business student as part of his industrial training with the aim of promoting certain power tool brand names, becoming a recognized distributor for suppliers, and dealing mainly with account customers. Initial operations were centred on retail premises.

Constraints

Cyril Turner was severely hampered by his previous employment at Brent Power Tools and by the existing power tools distribution system.

(a) Power tool companies and fixing suppliers generally only trade through distributors. Brent Power Tools Ltd already acted as the local distributor for many firms in the area and the manufacturers were unwilling to cause disruption and uncertainty in the market by encouraging an unknown factor in the shape of Turner Power Tools. The contacts that Turner had made while at Brent Power Tools were therefore effectively closed at the time of setting up his business.

(b) Turner had signed an agreement with Brent Power Tools undertaking not to approach their customers with the same products for a period of six months.

(c) The more reputable, well-established companies in the North London area already had distributors in the area; those manufacturers willing to sell through Turner Power Tools were unknown even in the trade with a product quality that was also unknown.

(d) Turner's intention of dealing with reputable power tool companies required greater cash outlay in holding stocks.

Options

(a) Many start-up businesses in the power tools market begin by buying and selling to order, depending on picking up any item and make of goods available. This, however, would affect the company's initial intention of dealing with reputable power tool manufacturers.

(b) The prospects for Turner Tools beginning by operating as a retail outlet was extremely limited since the equipment concerned consisted essentially of industrial tools made of hard-wearing parts to withstand heavy duty use whether on a building site or as part of a hire fleet. They are therefore about four times the price of an equivalent DIY tool.

(c) The Japanese manufacturer Sanaa was a newcomer to the UK power tools market. The company had made its name in electronic equipment, was well known and had a high reputation for reliability. Their power tools were proven excellent but as yet this section of the company had no distributor in the north and west of London. Turner Power Tools secured this Sanaa distributorship adding substantially to its image. As part of the agreement, Sanaa passed on to the distributor any enquiries about power tools in the area; in return Turner actively promoted the Sanaa equipment. Initially the company stocked about £3,000 of Sanaa tools; this subsequently increased to about 120 tools with a net value of about £9,000. By holding stock of Sanaa equipment Turner Power Tools soon found itself in a position to supply its competitors with Sanaa goods for them to re-sell.

Finding customers

Cyril Turner's potential customers included local government bodies, building and construction firms, joiner's shops, electricians, and maintenance departments. The trade tends to demand on-site personal service, being on hand to take orders and arrange the delivery of goods when required.

The demand for personal selling was reflected in an initial experiment. Turner's assistant sent a mail shot to all of the 40 names of approved builders on a list supplied by the council. They reasoned that most of those on the list were small firms working from home who would be difficult to contact otherwise and could ideally be canvassed through the post. They were also locally based so the mail shot would at least supply them with information about the new company. However, the mail shot generated no direct response. A similar result came from placing an advert in two local newspapers in consecutive weeks.

The trade was found to be a close knit one in which personal relationships with clients are very important. The price of goods is often less significant than the quality of the personal service offered: being on hand, supplying a good service including the willingness to supply goods at short notice, sometimes on the day the order is placed. In any case, customers expected deliveries within one to two days, with the sales representative often taking the goods to his own customers. Turner Power Tools were in addition willing to supply customers' requests for goods like specialist engineering tools which are not normally stocked. For those customers, such as the local authority which is only interested in price, the company was willing to match the prices quoted by competitors.

Progress

In the first three months of trading sales were double the figures expected (*see* Table 12.1). By the beginning of the fourth month of trading Turner found more and more of his time spent in the office dealing with customer enquiries and telephoned orders. As the enquiries became more complex it was essential that someone with good knowledge of the tool and fixing trade should be on hand to deal with telephone sales enquiries. It had become necessary to recruit a sales representative, someone to deal with telephone enquiries, and a clerk hired on the Youth Opportunities Scheme to process orders and take in suppliers' deliveries.

Table 12.1. Turner Power Tools sales and purchases 1983–84

Month	*Sales*	*Purchases*
November '83	3,308	2,401
December	4,078	6,181
January '84	10,627	5,142
February	18,306	8,941
March	14,803	13,498
April	13,679	9,887
May	21,064	11,407
June	19,583	6,952
July	30,204	10,536
August	20,555	32,378*
September	26,684	4,425
October	27,408	10,687
November	27,008	34,401*
December	15,395	19,593
Total	252,702	176,429

*Distortion caused by payments made for VAT quarter.

Paperwork

As sales increased so did the paperwork:

(a) Turner's customers placed small orders frequently. There were about 120 account customers and at the end of the month a statement was drawn up for each account. With no ledger system the statements were based on the sales day book and the difficulty in balancing the total outstanding at the end of each month had been increasing. It took between three and four days to prepare the balance statement each month.

(b) Turner's supplied a very wide range of goods, many of which were not held in house but subsequently ordered from suppliers. The increased use of this mechanism also greatly increased the number of delivery notes, invoices, and statements coming in from a large number of different suppliers – the company dealt with about 70, the majority of which would be involved in each month's trading.

Invoices had to be matched to delivery notes and all prices, discounts, and mathematical extensions checked; these all had to match the statements. As with sales there was no purchase ledger, but neither was there a purchase day book. To ensure that all payments for a certain month were made reliance was placed on memory and checking through all the invoices in the files.

(c) Each month's sales were based on the sales day book and this supplied the company's VAT analysis for sales. As there was no purchase day book the monthly VAT was calculated on the basis of cheque stubs and invoices marked paid for the month in question.

Case 2: Lockitt Fasteners

Lockitt Fasteners was a distributor of industrial fasteners dealing in nuts, rivets and washers, employing 11 people and had a turnover of £1.18 million in 1983. The nut side of the business was by far the largest and the company had invested in cold-forging plant enabling it to manufacture a good proportion of its nuts. The company had manufacturer-suppliers in a number of countries in the Far East, Eastern Europe, West Germany and Norway. Lockitt also sold in Europe as well as in the UK, its main customers being bolt manufacturers and other distributors, 25 per cent of them overseas.

In 1985 Lockitt, which had been trading for about eight years, had about 5.5 per cent of the nut market, but its sales over 1979–83 had decreased as had the total market. It was estimated that the overall market had contracted by 28 per cent since 1979 (*see* Table 12.2). In addition the total number of companies in the UK fastener market had declined from 720 in 1979 to 370 in 1983. In 1981 and 1983, when Lockitt made losses of £18,000 and £60,000 respectively, hefty sums of capital – £113,000 and £68,000 – were invested in the company.

The company realized that the market was contracting and its accountants now prepared the full external accounts on a half-yearly basis, which enabled Lockitt to monitor its progress in the middle of the financial year and review or adjust its strategy where appropriate. The company also prepared its own month-end profit and loss statement and also reviewed the yearly budget at the end of each month.

Since 1981 the company had trebled the number of customers, partly due to its promotional activities. Following losses in 1981 and 1983 the company tried to reduce expenses to achieve a lower break-even point, improve its sales and get the gross margins on its products up.

Table 12.2. UK fastener market in areas relevant to Lockitt (£'000)

Product	1979	1980	1981	1982	1983
Nuts	38,446	28,681	24,412	22,009	20,465
Rivets	38,654	38,216	33,661	35,171	38,745
Washers	20,154	13,966	12,656	12,337	12,088

General price levels had hardly changed in recent years forcing Lockitt to try to keep costs down. Whereas the company's manufacturer-suppliers also had to keep their prices down to remain competitive, Lockitt estimated that its own manufacturing costs had risen at about the same rate as inflation. Lockitt priced its products not on the basis of cost but according too how high a price the market would stand. This tended to mean that the gross margins on each product varied throughout the year.

Very nearly every new delivery from overseas for a particular product line differed in price to the previous one. In addition Lockitt had been unable to apportion costs such as rent, heating, lighting and so on to either the manufacturing or distribution operations for each product line.

Lockitt's sales in nuts had not decreased over the five year period as much as the actual nut segment had contracted (*see* Table 12.3). Sales in nuts decreased by 22.4 per cent but the nut segment of the UK fastener market contracted by 46.8 per cent.

All of Lockitt's account customers traded on a credit basis with the company and in 1983 the average payback period was 107 days, reduced from 122 days in 1981. Lockitt, by contrast, was in 1983 paying its creditors within 76 days of purchase.

Table 12.3. Lockitt's sales 1979–83 (£'000)

Product	1979	1980	1981	1982	1983
Nuts	1,447	1,278	1,302	1,259	1,123
Rivets	61	54	55	53	47
Washers	8	7	7	7	6

Lockitt Accounts 1979–83

	1979 £'000	1980 £'000	1981 £'000	1982 £'000	1983 £'000
Fixed assets	24	35	30	38	52
Stocks	216	273	226	252	288
Debtors	480	261	457	409	345
Total assets	731	582	725	710	688
Current liabilities	649	449	612	581	620
Capital employed	82	133	113	129	68
Total liabilities	731	582	725	710	688
Sales	1 523	1 345	1 370	1 325	1 182
Pre-tax profit (loss)	56	51	(18)	16	(60)
Exports	321	326	343	351	296
Profitability % Profit/Total assets	7.7	8.7	–ve	2.3	–ve
Profit margin % Profit/Sales	3.7	3.8	–ve	1.2	–ve
Capital usage (:1) Sales: Total assets	2.1	2.3	1.9	1.9	1.7
ROCE % Profit/Capital employed	68.3	38.3	–ve	12.4	–ve

Liquidity (:1) Current assets: Current liabilities	1.1	1.2	1.2	1.2	1.0
Stock turnover (:1) Sales: Stock	7.1	4.9	6.1	5.3	4.1
Credit period (days) Debtors/Sales × 365	115	71	122	113	107
Export ratio (:1) Export: Sales	2.1	2.4	2.5	2.6	2.5

Case 3: Funding Ebony Girl

In the search to attract funding a company called Ebony Girl approached one of the major clearing banks in South London for a start-up loan. It was seeking to establish a British company which would supply make-up manufactured especially for women of Afro-Caribbean origins who were currently buying imported make-up developed for black American women. A detailed business plan had been sent to the bank manager who was about to give it a thorough examination before making any further decision.

Summary of the Ebony Girl business plan

The Ebony Girl business plan supplied information and forecasts on the company's proposal to manufacture and distribute Afro-Caribbean make-up throughout the UK. It anticipated that sales would total £500,000 in the first year with profits in the region of £40,000. Sales in the final months of the first year would amount to about £70,000 a month, the plan said.

Expansion would continue in the second year with the introduction of new products as market penetration increased.

The Ebony Girl cash flow forecast indicated an initial requirement of £87,000 to finance the business start-up. This would be made up as follows:

	£
Owner capital	2,500
Outside investor	10,000
Bank loan	75,000

The market

The Afro-Caribbean make-up market began to expand in the UK about seven years previously, the products being tailor made to suit black skin types. The business plan estimated the value of the market at about £18 million, the end-user being women in the 18–30 age group. The centre of this market is in the Greater London area where Ebony Girl would initially concentrate its activities before expanding into the Midlands area.

The market is currently dominated by American companies selling through chemists and ethnic beauty salons. About 90 per cent of the ethnic type of make-up sold in the UK is imported from the USA. The products are expensive both as make-up and in comparison to similar products of the same quality for white women. Furthermore, the image of these products as sold in the UK is strongly American showing little appreciation of the cultural distinctiveness of the Afro-Caribbean heritage. The limited market research carried out by Ebony Girl indicated that there was a market gap for a product that is slightly cheaper than the main competitors at the top end of the market but still significantly more expensive than the cheaper end of the market. The company intended to offer products of similar, or slightly better quality than those of the up-market competition.

Local manufacturers would produce and package Ebony Girl products according to its own specifications. The products would be distributed from a small warehouse in London initially to about 100 chemists and beauty salons and about 10 wholesalers.

Ebony Girl's marketing

In the month before the launch of the Ebony Girl beauty pack – comprising a face colour foundation in three shades, lip colour in four shades, blusher in two shades, and eye colour in three shades – two salespeople would approach beauty salons and retail outlets with samples, promotional aids and literature on the products and offering discounts on first purchases.

The target group of 18–30 year olds would be reached through advertisements in Chic and Root magazines and advertisements on

London Transport Buses and Solar Radio during the first year. Adverts in the first month would introduce the product; in the second month they would be accompanied by coupons giving discounts on various lines.

In that month 12 young women would also promote the products in shopping centres, handing out samples and leaflets with product details.

Wholesalers would be sent information about Ebony Girl and a marketing package supplying details on the adverts and promotions. This would be followed up with a meeting to discuss the support they would receive from the company.

Personnel and premises

The company is owned and managed by Samuel Thomas, a former salesman with experience in marketing and computing. He is responsible for sales to wholesalers, promotions and marketing and advertising. Two other managers deal with stock and distribution and sales. Ebony Girl also has a part-time book-keeper and a part-time secretary.

In the plan the company indicated that it would have a warehouse in South-East London with an annual rental of £224 per month exclusive of all outgoings to be paid monthly in advance. Outgoings – security and cleaning – amount to £64 per month. The warehouse would be close to the major wholesalers in the market.

Cash flow forecast

The assumption used in the cash flow forecast given below was to achieve an immediate 1 per cent market penetration. Ebony Girl further anticipated that after a period of six months a 2 per cent penetration would be realistically achievable. A further assumption is that whilst wholesalers will be given 60 days' credit, an average of 90 days will be taken, even after accepting strict credit control procedures. The company would be seeking to factor its invoices in month five for a period of at least six months. This would enable the company to obtain 80 per cent of invoices for that month at a cost of 3 per cent above overdraft base rate, with the remaining 20 per cent to be paid under normal credit terms.

Ebony Girl cash flow forecast

Month	1	2	3	4	5	6	7	8	9	10	11	12
RECEIPTS												
Credit sales				17250	44850	44850	48300	75900	48300	65550	65550	65550
Owners capital	2500											
Investors capital	10000											
Loan	75000											
VAT Refund					692			0			0	
TOTAL RECEIPTS	87500	0	0	17250	45542	44850	48300	75900	48300	65550	65550	65550

PAYMENTS												
Suppliers	21411		6389	12777	15972	15972	23958	23958	23958	31944	31944	31944
Light & heat	0	0	0	1000	0	0	1000	0	0	1000	0	0
Telephone	0	0	0	690	0	0	690	0	0	690	0	0
Print & post	6000	150	150	350	150	150	350	150	150	350	150	150
Advertising	2120	7670	6550	6550	2250	2250	6550	6550	6550	6550	6550	6550
Legal & prof	1000	1000				690						1150
Travel & rent	250	250	250	250	250	250	250	250	250	250	250	250
Motor I	550	550	550	550	550	550	550	550	650	650	650	650
Finance charges	1175	519	519	519	519	519	519	519	519	519	519	519
Sales wages inc NI	663	663	663	663	663	663	663	663	663	663	663	663
Salaries inc NI	2574	2574	2574	2574	2574	2574	2574	2574	2574	2574	2574	2574
Rent & rates	909	284	734	1359	734	734	1359	734	734	1359	734	734
Office equipment	750	0	0	0	0	1500	0	200	0	200	0	200
Loan charges/ repayment	1250	1250	1250	1250	1250	1250	2640	2640	2640	2640	2640	2640
Factoring interest					345	690	1207	1379	1551	1724	1897	2070
Factoring charges						907	907	907	907	907	907	907
Insurance	3000											
VAT payments				0			19264			29978		
TOTAL PAYMENTS	41652	14910	19629	28532	25257	28699	62481	41074	41146	81998	49478	51001
NET INFLOW/ OUTFLOW	45848	-14910	-19629	-11282	20285	16151	-14181	34826	7154	-16448	16072	14549
OPENING BALANCE	0	45848	30938	11309	27	20312	36463	22282	57108	64262	47814	63886
CLOSING BALANCE	45848	30938	11309	27	20312	36463	22282	57108	64262	47814	63886	78435
LOWEST BALANCE IN MONTH	0	0	0	0	0	0	0	0	0	0	0	0
Invoiced sales	17250	17250	17250	34500	34500	34500	51750	51750	51750	69000	69000	69000

Ebony Girl Trading and Profit and Loss Account for end of first period

	£	£
Turnover		450,000
Cost of sales		208,893
Gross profit		241,107
Overhead expenditure		
Salaries	38,844	
Rent & rates	10,408	
Light & heat	3,000	
Telephone	2,070	
Insurance	3,000	
Advertising & promotions	66,690	
Printing, postage, stationery	8,250	
Legal & professional	3,840	
Office equipment	2,850	
Travelling & entertainment	3,000	
Motor expenses	7,000	
Sundry expenses	–	
Interest & finance charges	47,436	
		196,388
Net profit before tax		£44,719

Trade and sundry creditors

	£
Trade creditors (1 month)	31,944
Salaries (1 month)	3,237
Light & heat (1 quarter)	1,000
Telephone (1 quarter)	600
	£36,781
Trade debtors 20% of factored invoices	41,400

12

Case 4: Ceres Interior Art Limited

Robert Wright had before him the accounts of Ceres Interior Art Limited, a company specializing in high quality frieze and interior art and design work. Wright had a substantial amount of money which he was willing to invest in a small company under the right circumstances but was particularly concerned to ensure that he gained a measure of control in the company involved in return for his investment. Apart from the knowledge that the company urgently needed a substantial injection of cash, the current owner and manager of Ceres was ambivalent about the terms that would be acceptable to him. Wright was therefore giving thought to size of the offer he would make to the company in return for complete control over its operations.

The Ceres profit and loss accounts

	1984		1983	
	£	£	£	£
Turnover		238,062		203,473
Materials	51,649		17,462	
Wages and sub-contractors	162,353		115,745	
Consultants fees	3,250		–	
Quantity surveyors fees	7,933		–	
		225,185		133,207
Gross profit		12,877		70,266
Expenses				
Establishment	4,047		2,289	
Administration	16,807		5,568	
Selling	26,300		25,240	
Financial	14,502		9,608	
Depreciation	6,391		5,143	
		68,047		47,848
(Loss)/Profit		(55,170)		22,418
Rent received		3,150		3,150
		(52,020)		25,568
Extraordinary item		5,601		–
		(46,419)		25,568

Ceres expenses

The Ceres expenses for the year ended 31 September 1984 were as follows:

	1984		1983	
	£	£	£	£
Establishment				
Rent and rates	2,286		591	
Heat and light	1,761		1,698	
		4,047		2,289
Administration				
Telephone	2,597		2,486	
Equipment hire	2,113		1,018	
Postage/stationery	1,662		641	
Accountancy	9,678		800	
Repairs/renewals	329		290	
Sundries	428		333	
		16,807		5,568
Selling				
Bad debts	–		2,500	
Commission	–		253	
Meals/accommodation	3,103		3,576	
Advertising	11,671		6,271	
Transport	9,487		11,093	
Insurance	2,039		1,547	
		26,300		25,240
Financial				
Loan interest	1,710		3,662	
Rentals under leases	4,051		4,218	
Bank interest/charges	7,109		1,110	
Hire purchase interest	1,632		618	
		14,502		9,608
Depreciation		6,391		5,143
		68,047		47,848

The Ceres balance sheet

The Ceres balance sheet at the end of September 1984 looked like this:

	1984		1983	
	£	£	£	£
Fixed assets		108,011		58,956
Goodwill		1,000		1,000
Current assets				
Stock	44,625		57,024	
Debtors	17,146		7,558	
Building society	–		396	
Hire purchase interest	2,143		2,053	
	£63,914		£67,031	
Current liabilities				
Bank overdraft	106,110		28,277	
Creditors	38,334		6,106	
Loan	–		5,045	
Hire purchase accounts	13,110		22,405	
Merchant bank loan			23,462	
	£170,134		£95,487	
Net current liabilities		(106,220)		(28,546)
		£2,791		£31,500
Capital		2,791		31,500

Case 5: Cannon Studios

In 1985 Arthur Bell decided that to establish his commercial photographic work firmly he needed to purchase a studio in which he could photograph kitchen furniture, large industrial equipment, and complete catalogue work. After much investigation, he managed to find a large old tithe barn which appeared to be eminently suitable for the task in hand. After approaching the local bank, he was able to raise £90,000 for the purchase of the property while putting in £90,000 himself from the sale of his house.

The overheads that were involved in the operation were:

Loan interest	£12,600
Capital repayment	£2,600
Rates	£1,000
Wages (assistant)	£4,000
Living expenses	£3,000
Heating/lighting	£750
Hire of equipment	£3,000
Telephone	£550
Misc.	£650

The income that would be generated by the operation included the sub-letting of part of the tithe barn, around £4,000 per annum, and commercial photographic work which would generate around £350 per day.

Popular commercial photographers manage to spend around 50 per cent of their week actually working, the remainder finding and developing projects. Such a workload takes years to generate and Arthur Bell was finding that only 25 per cent of his week was fully occupied.

Looking at the budget he was wondering whether the business based in the large studio was viable and what else he could do to generate additional business.

Case 6: XYZ Wholesale Foods

The UK cash and carry food distribution industry has changed over the past 25 years and is dominated by relatively few companies. Ten companies accounted for 50 per cent of the sector's valued sales in 1984, with all but three either maintaining or improving their market position. With low bargaining power over suppliers many of the small companies like XYZ Wholesale Foods have been forced out of business. Some have been compelled to form groups simply in order to gain volume discounts and good trading terms from manufacturers.

Table 12.4 shows that the cash and carry industry has had over 60 per cent of the UK grocery wholesalers trade since the beginning of the decade. Expansion has been continuous from 61 per cent in 1980 to 66 per cent in 1983, increasing by 10 per cent in 1984. Nevertheless annual growth has persistently declined. Thus in 1972 there was a 34 per cent increase in sales over 1971 but by 1984 the percentage sales increase over 1983 was 10 per cent.

The industry

Table 12.4. UK grocery trade (£m) 1980–83

Year	*Total sales*	*Cash & carry*	*Market share %*	*Delivered trade*	*Market share %*
1980	3,750	2,305	61	1,445	39
1981	4,989	3,166	63	1,823	37
1982	5,192	3,356	65	1,836	35
1983	5,593	3,685	66	1,908	34

Given the concentration and rationalization for one-stop shopping, the need for large financial resources for entry is obvious. Companies with favourable locations and access to manufacturers enjoy the advantages of good trading terms through volume purchase. There is also cumulative experience accruing to established firms in terms of distribution, but the most conspicuous economies of scale lie in large warehouses offering one-stop shopping. The advent of microprocessor systems may ultimately constitute a major deterrent in an industry that is currently regarded as relatively unsophisticated since they will affect areas of inventory planning and control as product lines and range continue to increase.

Although the industry is not production oriented there has been a substantial increase in the own-brand trade of the top ten companies in their attempts to offer competitive prices and consumer loyalty (*see* Table 12.5).

Table 12.5. Cash and carry own-label lines

Company	*Brand names*	*Approx. no. of lines*
Linfood	Hallmark	375
ICCG	Sterling	309
N&P	Peacock	300
Lonsdale	ShopLocal	230
Makro	Aro	200
Consort	Consort	195
	Our Generic	50
Keencost	Maytree	150
Booker	Family Choice	100
Batleys	Batleys	60

Generally the cash and carry industry is so fragmented that its buyers exert little or no influence over their suppliers. The large number of buyers, contrasted with the limited number of suppliers, gives individual companies little bargaining power because of low volume purchase. With the major exception of the large companies or those in voluntary groups buying in larger volumes, most individual companies are unable to exert any influence on suppliers partly because the industry does not represent a significant fraction of the suppliers' sales.

The main source of indirect competition comes from the giant multiple retailers and from retail buying groups such as Links by-passing the cash and carry and buying directly from suppliers in order to gain volume discounts from bulk purchasing. Recent trends indicate quite clearly that independents, specialists and small operators in general are progressively losing their share of the market to the multiple grocery chain retailers thereby affecting the growth potential in the cash and carry industry. There is therefore increasing competition for market shares as companies suffer negative or declining profits. Buyer discrimination has led to increased competitive emphasis on cost and service.

The grocery market showed a number of clear trends:

(a) There was a steady increase in the amount of frozen food (per capita consumption of frozen vegetables had for example increased from 0.9 kg per annum in 1979 to 3.5 in 1985).

(b) The amount of convenience food purchased was steadily increasing.

(c) There was a movement towards larger packs of all items.

(d) Sales of alcohol continued to grow, especially wine, up from 8 litres in 1979 to 11 litres in 1985 per capita.

(e) Confectionery and tobacco sales continue to show a slow decline.

XYZ Wholesale Foods

XYZ Wholesale Foods, a distributive trade company, is a family run private limited company with three warehouses in London. It employs about 40 people but has no formal organizational structure, top management being heavily involved in day-to-day running operations. The company began trading in 1976 and succeeded in achieving rapid growth at a time when the cash and carry industry was beginning to experience a steady contraction in growth. After a leap from £2 million sales in 1980 to £15 million in 1982, real growth has consistently declined.

With nearly 330 accounts, all XYZ products are sold through the three warehouses which offer similar product lines competitively priced. Its customers are mainly drink/CTNs and grocery outlets. Promotion is via a mail shot sent out at three weekly intervals containing details of special offers.

The three warehouses, situated in good locations, are open six days a week from 9 a.m. to 8 p.m. However, exits and entrances are poorly designed and customers wheeling trolleys sometimes find it difficult to avoid accidents. Further evidence of poor design is also evident within the warehouses where display signs are substandard.

The profit margin had historically remained low at 1 per cent of turnover. This was, however, higher than some of its other competitors, though margin on sales in grocery retailing traditionally held at 4–5 per cent.

It was estimated that the current company turnover and profit figures were as follows:

12

Item	*% Turnover*	*% Profit*
Basic grocery	60	67
Fresh vegetables	10	6
Catering packs	15	13
Frozen	3	5
Alcohol	8	11
Tobacco	4	–2

Services and customers

A survey of wholesalers and retailers was carried out in the London area to identify the opportunities available to XYZ. The findings revealed that food represented 52 per cent of wholesalers' trade of which confectionery, grocery and provisions were the most important items. Indeed the cash and carry trade continues to concentrate stock in the traditional areas of general groceries and provisions, confectionery, cigarettes and tobacco. There is, however, a trend towards non-food products partly due to developments in the shopping for convenience environment.

The survey revealed that the wholesalers' main customers were drink/CTN and grocers who together accounted for 90 per cent of turnover of the 14 companies surveyed. Catering outlets represented 50 per cent of the turnover of 10 companies.

Customers on average travelled up to six miles to visit the cash and carry twice a week. Of these, 65 per cent of drink/CTN and grocery outlets purchased between £400 and £800 of goods in an average week. The purchasing patterns of caterers, public houses and off-licences showed a greater degree of fluctuation in purchasing patterns.

Certain types of retailers do not use a cash and carry: sellers of fresh and specialist foods, hardware/electrical, pet and toy shops, gift shops, florists, stationery and printing establishments. They use either specialist discount warehouses, or direct purchase from suppliers, relying only on the cash and carry for odd items.

Given the advantages enjoyed by the large retailing chains, pricing was relatively less important to cash and carry customers when compared with the service potential. A good location – customers did not want to have to travel any great distance to the cash and carry – a wide range of goods, product availability, late/early and/or seven day opening and delivery were all more important than price to the CTN/grocers, caterers, and public house/off-licences. Credit and special offers were also regarded as being less important.

A further insight provided by the survey which is relevant to perceptions on price was the finding that nearly 80 per cent of the retailer outlets involved also buy directly from delivery wholesalers or from manufacturers, while 15 per cent of CTN/grocery outlets and 33 per cent of caterers purchase from large multiple retailers for re-sale alongside direct supply. In this context product availability, convenience, lower prices and the credit offered by non cash and carry sources were important influences.

Case 7: Pineapple Records

Background

The popular recording industry is dominated by six major companies that make up over 60 per cent of the market. These companies generally cater for established groups: those that already command an audience and are guaranteed sales through the major outlets.

There are in addition an enormous number of independent record labels that concentrate on minor artists and groups. By the late 1970s over 3,000 of these were in existence.

Pineapple

The concept behind Pineapple was to provide a service for artists wishing to record music without resorting to the independent labels by sub-contracting the recording, label design and production, and offering an overall lower price than competitive record labels. Margins would be low as Pineapple would exist primarily on additional discounts that it could arrange from the various production units, but it was hoped that with the potentially large market for such a broking service, the company would be rapidly profitable. The long-term plan involved the purchase of their own recording studios at an estimated cost of £35,000. An example of how the Pineapple approach would work can be seen in this example for the production of 1,000 records in plain covers:

12

	Normal price	*Pineapple*
Recording	£400	£325
Editing	£80	£60
Pressing	£300	£225
Printing	£150	£100
Promotion	£200	£120

Distribution was to be achieved through a major record wholesaler, and promotion was via a newsletter to 'opinion makers' in the industry.

Financial forecast:

Item	*1984*	*1985*
Sales	£40,000	£80,000
Cash outflow	£49,000	£62,000
Capital	£1,500	£1,500

The actual results were far less encouraging. By 1985 only 5 records had been pressed and turnover was struggling at the £10,000 area.

The company had identified several major areas of weakness:

(a) *Promotion*. The world of record promotion was very insular with a small number of record promoters having a central role in the acquiring of air time for any record (70 per cent of records are bought after being heard on the radio). Pineapple were finding it difficult with limited finances to break into this market.

(b) *Competition*. The large number of competitive studios made access to new artists very difficult. This had a particularly acute affect on the distribution channel as the large numbers of competitive labels handled by the distributor reduced the time that each record could receive.

(c) *Financial backing*. The lack of financial backing required Pineapple to pay cash for all items; it also lowered their standing when attempting to gain new clients.

(d) *Quality*. Though the record quality was consistent with the normal industry standard, the sub-contracting approach and the low cost route chosen often left customers dissatisfied with the final product when compared with the obviously more expensive approach of the independent studio.

The future

The two owners of Pineapple studio were unhappy with current progress and were attempting to define a future strategy.

Appendix: computer Spreadsheet packages

A computer Spreadsheet package can be a very useful tool when developing a business plan for a small business. This appendix is intended to show how a Spreadsheet is used and how it can help planning.

Using a Spreadsheet

The package

There is nothing mystifying about a computer Spreadsheet package. It offers the user a simple, blank table divided by verticals and horizontals into boxes – described in the jargon as 'cells' – ready to receive the user's numerical information and using that data to make quick calculations by means of simple mathematical formulae also supplied by the user.

Advantages of the Spreadsheet

A most important feature of the Spreadsheet, which gives it a unique advantage over manual systems, is that it enables the user to have immediate access to the likely effect of changing even a single number. When one alters a value in a sequence of calculations the Spreadsheet will automatically calculate its impact on the whole sequence. This obviously means that the Spreadsheet is particularly useful as a business planning tool because it can supply a rapid demonstration of cause and effect – what would happen to a business' profits, for example, if sales increased or decreased by five per cent over the planning horizon.

In addition, the size of the Spreadsheet table means that it is possible to compare and contrast an enormous amount of data. An average Spreadsheet computer software package will cope with a cash budget, pro forma income statement, and pro forma balance sheet. When they are linked by formulae on the Spreadsheet a change in any of the major items on the cash budget will instantly be reflected in changes on the other two. Whether the figures for total sales, inventory costs, or overhead costs have been altered, the Spreadsheet will enable you to see the effect of the changes on your cash position and profitability.

The software

The first step is to create a correctly operating system on the computer Spreadsheet. That involves becoming familiar with the idiosyncracies of the particular software that you are using. This will not necessarily be an easy task, and it will require a great deal of concentration, for example transferring numbers onto a computer is always time consuming and laborious. Furthermore, you will have to be absolutely accurate in the numbers and formulae you input. More often than not, you will also have to become familiar with any quirks in the software package as well as in the computer system. Yet there is a great deal of satisfaction to be gained in seeing the Spreadsheet operating and once the system is working then the task is more or less over. Further modifications and changing data will present only minor problems.

Spreadsheets such as the Lotus 123, VisiCalc and SuperCalc are available for practically all computer systems and they share a variety of standard features. The Spreadsheet exercises given here can be used with any Spreadsheet system and will adapt to new systems such as Framework and Symphony. All have a Value Option which handles the numbers and calculation formulae, and a Label Option to identify the data. The functions used for calculation in the exercises are: * = multiply; / = divide; + = add; – = subtract.

An important function that appears frequently in Spreadsheet calculations is the 'IF' command. This is always followed by a mathematical statement, for example: 'IF(B1 = 9) true (X), false (Y)'. This varies in the exact form it takes in different Spreadsheets. It is presented in this book in the standard form 'IF B = 9 THEN (VALUE) ELSE (VALUE)' as this format is more understandable for the model builder.

The building of each model is explained on a cell-by-cell basis. As you gain experience with the Spreadsheet system a number of cells can be replicated to other cells using commands which vary with the Spreadsheet system. Learning these techniques will reduce considerably the labour involved in transferring the Spreadsheet exercises given here onto your computer.

Perhaps the best way of understanding how the Spreadsheet can be used as a planning tool is to take an example from scratch. This we shall do in the next section.

An introductory exercise: competitive bidding

Within the business environment the organization faces a large number of constraints on distribution, production and the like. In a free market, however, it does normally have the ability to set its prices and its costs at whatever level it wants (providing of course that this is a coherent decision, enabling profitability to be maintained). There are two exceptions to this general statement, both relating to one-off events: the wage bargaining process and the sealed bidding system in operation for major capital projects. Both of these activities operate in an environment which is largely isolated from both the market and the underlying cost constraints. In other words, the process at work is very similar to betting, each particular bet (price point) having associated odds (probability of occurrence) and possible winnings (consequent profitability/cost effect).

Thus for both wage negotiation and sealed bidding the organization needs to determine the *value* of each level of bid and the *profit* or cost of each level of decision. From this the most cost-effective approach can be developed, which should maximize the firm's position over the long-term. Naturally, other constraints may be more important; for example the firm may choose to pay their employees more than the suggested level of wage settlement because of changes in the working environment, or it may choose to complete a contract at marginal cost to gain access to new markets, as a form of introductory pricing.

The factors involved

The Spreadsheet exercise will provide a convenient framework in which alternative strategies may be evaluated rapidly. Price is the proposed range of bid values, ranging from the lowest to the highest price that could be feasibly attained. Cost is the underlying cost associated with the bid, similar in each case, and an ideal opportunity to develop a marginal costing system. The organization would also need to consider the implications of opportunity costing, especially important in one-off bids. For the wage negotiation, the cost will obviously be the same as the bid price. Lastly, the probability that each bid can be successful should be assigned for each event occurring. The range of probability, with 100 comprising certainty that the bid will be successful, should be considered by each of the managers responsible, so that the best group consensus can be arrived at. The higher the price the lower the probability of success will be. The model will compare the level of probability with the expected profitability at differing pricing levels, allowing the most cost-effective mix of price and probability to be developed. Obviously the probability of success will be a subjective assessment involving experience of the market conditions, competitors' pricing levels, and any special factor that may exist (foreign exchange problems for example).

Applying the model to the Spreadsheet

Using a step-by-step approach, let us apply the model based on the principles discussed above to a Spreadsheet system. This will teach you the practicalities of using the system and will help you to assess the arguments for and against a particular course of action.

Before you begin you will have loaded your Spreadsheet system into the computer.

All the instructions to the computer are placed between inverted commas to help you to pick them out at a glance, but as they are not part of the instructions they should not be typed on the keyboard! Beware that some Spreadsheets, the Lotus 123 for example, enter the Label Option by using the inverted comma key.

1. Load the Spreadsheet and have it before you on the screen. The GoTo column tells you the cell number and the cursor position. The next column specifies the Spreadsheet option [LO = Label Option; VO = Value Option]. The Type In column gives you instructions within the inverted commas which you must type in or asks you to supply the necessary data. R for Return instructs you to commit the information to memory by pressing the Return key.

2. Move the cursor to cell B2 and choose the Label Option. Type 'Competit' on the status line and enter into memory by pressing the Return key. 'Competit' will appear in cell B2 in the body of the Spreadsheet. This last, described here in order to familiarize you with what to expect when you are using a Spreadsheet, will take place automatically on pressing the return key and will be taken as read for the subsequent instructions. Note that you will have to type the remainder of the word 'Competitive' in cell C2.

3. When you choose the Value Option (VO) the information entered will be used for calculation purposes. The Value Option also includes the whole range of equations provided for the model. When you select the Value Option and type in the values or equation in the model the Spreadsheet follows the procedure you have decided upon. For example, if you have located the cursor at, say, cell E83 and you type in C10*A15 the Spreadsheet will multiply the values in those two cells together and the answer will appear in cell E83 on the screen. Thus if the value of C10 was 5 and the value of A15 was 3 the result in the cell E83 would be 15. **Note: * = multiply; / = divide.**

Go To		Type In	RReturn
B2/	LO	"COMPETITIVE	R
C2/	–	BIDDING	R
D2/	–	MODEL"	R
E2	–	–	R
A6	LO	"PRICE"	R
C6	LO	"COST"	R
D6	LO	"% PROBAB" for Probability	R
E6	LO	"VALUE"	R
F6	LO	"EXP RET" for Expected Return	
A10	VO	Insert possible bidding price	$R
A12	VO	Insert second possible	R
–	–	bidding price	–
A14	VO	Insert third possible	R
–	–	bidding price	–
A16	VO	Insert fourth possible	R
–	–	bidding price	–
A18	VO	Insert fifth possible	R
–	–	bidding price	–
C10	VO	Insert cost of bid in A10	R
C12	VO	Insert cost of bid in A12	R
C14	VO	Insert cost of bid in A14	R
C16	VO	Insert cost of bid in A16	R
C18	VO	Insert cost of bid in A18	R
–	–	–	–

Note the estimated cost of C10–C18 will be similar in each case *because the production cost will be identical in each case*

D10	VO	Insert probability of	R
–	–	achieving respective target	–
–	–	price for A10	–

When price goes up probability of success goes down			
D12	VO	Insert probability of	R
–	–	achieving target price for A12	
D14	VO	Insert probability of	R
–	–	achieving target price for A14	
D16	VO	Insert probability of	R
–	–	achieving target price for A16	
D18	VO	Insert probability of	R
–	–	achieving target price for D18	
E10	VO	"A10–C10"	R
–	–	–	–
E12	VO	"A12–C12"	R
E14	VO	"A14–C14"	R
E16	VO	"A16–C16"	R
E18	VO	"A18–C18"	R
F10	VO	"E10*D10/100"	R
–	–	–	–
F12	VO	"E12*D12/100"	R
F14	VO	"E14*D14/100"	R
F16	VO	"E16*D16/100"	R
F18	VO	"E18*D18/100"	R

Remember: Save your exercise on disk; always keep a copy on another disk; as you work through the exercise save it onto the disk at regular intervals – this will help to minimize extra work if you are distracted, or if you have any problems with the computer.

Applying the other Spreadsheet models

Using the competitive bidding model (see Fig. A.1) as an example the other models can be entered into the Spreadsheet using the tables provided in Figs. A.2–A.5. These indicate the grid references to where the formula should be entered to develop the model; other data will need to be entered from the company's records.

Thus the marginal profitability model requires the planner to enter both planned volumes, prices and levels of proposed fixed costs and advertising expenditure to work out the overall rate of return.

A similar use of actual figures will be needed to compare past and current positions for the cash flow model.

	A	B	C	D	E	F
2		COMPETITIVE BIDDING MODEL				
6	PRICE		COST	%PROBAB	VALUE	EXP RET
10	1000000		900000	95	A10-C10	E10*D10/100
12	1050000		900000	85	A12-C12	E12*D12/100
14	1100000		900000	75	A14-C14	E14*D14/100
16	1150000		9000000	60	A16-C16	E16*D16/100
18	1200000		9000000	45	A18-C18	E18*D18/100

Fig. A.1 Competitive bidding model

Marginal profitability

The use of a Spreadsheet system which allows the maximum control over the variables involved in the costing procedure needs to take account of the direct and variable cost problems associated with each particular product line. Using the Spreadsheet model can aid the development of a system in which profit is the most important element in the equation, and not the recovery of overhead. The aims are to produce a *Profit and loss statement* for each product line.

The first necessity is to evaluate the level of costs which are always incurred by a particular product at any level of activity. For example, the production of powder detergents demands the use of a blowing tower so whatever happens the cost of maintaining that plant item will always be incurred by the powder detergent company.

Costs for a particular product as volume increases will not move in a linear fashion but tend to be a compound of a series of different factors.

Materials tend to become cheaper as volume utilization increases; labour unit costs remain linear, as do energy costs. Some other costs may increase in step fashion as each new level of volume brings in a complete unit of additional resource.

The summation of these lines occurs naturally within any company as demand either increases or decreases. Thus the company will have produced for each product line a graph of costs over a particular volume range. Regression analysis of this line will cross the cost line at a particular point, which can be termed the basic activity cost. This would be analogous to the costs continuing to be incurred during a strike for example.

As well as the specific base costs of a particular product there may be a series of expenditures which are general to the product range and which can only be allocated on that basis. To carry the analogy of the detergent powder further, packaging line costs can be specific, blowing tower depreciation would be general. For a profit and loss account these items should be included as below the line activities as they are standard expenses not relating to any particular activity level.

Similar considerations should apply to the development of advertising support, promotional activity, and finally any research and development expenditure relating to the specific product line.

Once these two areas have become established it is possible to consider specific areas of volume related pricing:

1. *Trade discounts.* These can be an important loss maker if margins are slim and total discounts are not controlled.

2. *Commissions.* Similarly, control over the amount of money that is being expended in commissions is important in the overall brand profitability.

3. Distribution costs. These will be particularly relevant if they constitute a large number of separate deliveries to customers and will require an individual line in any evaluation.

4. Direct materials. Here all the material cost relating to the product line should be included.

5. Direct labour. As for direct materials, all the material cost relating to the product line should be included.

6. Manufacturing expense. All the variable expenses associated with the production of the product.

7. Commercial expenses. This category includes all the overheads associated with the credit control department, personnel function and so on.

These figures will provide the total variable production cost directly relating to the particular product line.

8. Base costs. Those costs relating to the product at a shutdown level of activity, both at a general and specific level.

9. Line expenditure. This covers all advertising and research and development expenditure relating either in a general or specific fashion.

10. Capital employed. One of the important aspects of this model is to enable the manager to gain an understanding of the level of capital employed for each particular product line. This should be provided as an input for calculation, to develop the overall profit analysis as a return on capital employed and not in comparison with the budgeted figures of the previous year or a return on sales. This may reveal that a certain product, while being highly profitable in isolation, is requiring a high level of capital investment whereas other items in the range may easily show a higher return on investment albeit with a lower profit margin on sales price.

The major advantages that this system has are two-fold. First, it enables the budgeting to be simply changed without a total re-evaluation of the underlying basic costs in the product costings as these are fixed at all levels of production. Second, the model concentrates on the return on capital employed, which the majority of analyses tend to ignore but which is crucial to profit planning.

This model escapes the problems faced by overhead recovery systems, in that problems can be quickly identified and acted upon. It also avoids the difficulties of direct costing systems which do not include sufficient information concerning the basic costs that the company must continue to carry.

The main advantage to management is that they are presented with the same level of cost at any level of output which enable decisions to be reached easily without the complexity of coping with variations of cost at

A/B	C	D	E	F	G	H	I	K	L
4 Marginal	Profitability	Control							
10	Company	Line A	actual	variance	Line B	actual	variance	company	company
11								revised	variance
12 Volume		300000	277500	D12-E12	200000	200000	H12-G12		
13 Unit price $		20	20	D13-E13	20	21	H13-G13		
14 Sales $	D14+G14	D12*D13	E12*E13	D14-E14	G12*G13	H12*H13	H14-G14	E14+H14	K14-C14
16 Variable costs									
18 Discount$	D18+G18	250000	240000	D18-E18	300000	240000	G18-H18	E18+H18	C18-K18
20 Commissions$	D20+G20	205000	230000	D20-E20	150000	165000	G20-H20	E20+H20	C20-K20
22 Distribution$	D22+G22	40000	35000	D22-E22	35000	35000	G22-H22	E22+H22	C22-K22
24 Material$	D24+G24	2500000	2200000	D24-E24	1500000	1550000	G24-H24	E24+H24	C24-K24
26 Labour$	D26+G26	800000	720000	D26-E26	450000	475000	G26-H26	E26+H26	C26-K26
28 Manufacture$	D28+G28	125000	168000	D28-E28	100000	150000	G28-H28	E28+H28	C28-K28
30 TOTAL VARIABLE	SUM(C18;C28)	SUM(D18;D28)	SUM(E18;E28)	SUM(F18;F28)	SUM(G18;G28)	SUM(H18;H28)	SUM(I18;I28)	SUM(K18;K28)	SUM(L18;L28)
31 COST$									
33 TOTAL VARIABLE	C14-C30	D14-D30	E14-E30	F14+F30	G14-G30	H14-H30	I14+I30	K14-K30	L14+L30
34 PROFIT$									
36 BASE COSTS									
38 Specific	D38+G38	750000	750000	D38-E38	450000	450000	G38-H38	E38+H38	C38-K38
39 General	D39+G39	230000	230000	D39-E39	125000	125000	G39-H39	E39+H39	C39-K39
42 LINE EXP $									
44 Specific	D44+G44	230000	345000	D44-E44	150000	230000	G44-H44	E44+H44	C44-K44
45 General	D45+G45	112000	122000	D45-E45	42000	65000	G45-H45	E45+H45	C45-K45
48 TOTAL PROFIT $	D48+G48	D33-SUM(D38;D45)	E33-SUM(E38;E45)	F33+SUM(F38;F45)	G33-SUM(G38;G45)	H33-SUM(H38;H45)	I33+SUM(I38;I45)	K33-SUM(K38;K45)	L33+SUM(L38;L45)
50 CAPITAL	D50+G50	500000	500000	E50-D50	405000	430000	H50-G50	E50+H50	K50-C50
51 EMPLOYED									
53 RETURN ON CAP	C48/C50-1	D48/D50-1	E48/E50-1	IFE53>D53THEN10ELSE0	G48/G50-1	H48/H50-1	IF(H53>G53)THEN(10)ELSE(0)	K48/K50-1	IF(K53>C53)THEN(10)ELSE(0)
54 EMPLOYED									
55 Gross mg/unit		D33/D12	E33/E12		G33/G12	H33/H12			
56 Break even		SUM(D38;D45)/D55	SUM(E38;E45)/E55		SUM(G38;G45)/G55	SUM(H38;H45)/H55			

Fig. A.2 Marginal profitability

	A	B	C	D	E	F	G	H	I	J	K	L	M	N
2	MAT ANALYSIS													
4		MONTH 0	MONTH 1	MONTH 2	MONTH 3	MONTH 4	MONTH 5	MONTH 6	MONTH7	MONTH8	MONTH9	MONTH10	MONTH11	MONTH12
5	1	5000	5500	5500	5500	5500	5500	5500	5500	5500	5500	5500	5500	5500
6	2	2400	2400	3200	3200	3200	3200	3200	3200	3200	3200	3200	3200	3200
7	3	3400	3400	3400	3700	3700	3700	3700	3700	3700	3700	3700	3700	3700
8	4	4000	4000	4000	4000	4500	4500	4500	4500	4500	4500	4500	4500	4500
9	5	5000	5000	5000	5000	5000	6000	6000	6000	6000	6000	6000	6000	6000
10	6	4500	4500	4500	4500	4500	4500	5500	5500	5500	5500	5500	5500	5500
11	7	4790	4790	4790	4790	4790	4790	4790	7200	7200	7200	7200	7200	7200
12	8	4500	4500	4500	4500	4500	4500	4500	4500	3800	3800	3800	3800	3800
13	9	6000	6000	6000	6000	6000	6000	6000	6000	6000	4800	4800	4800	4800
14	10	7000	7000	7000	7000	7000	7000	7000	7000	7000	7000	7500	7500	7500
15	11	4000	4000	4000	4000	4000	4000	4000	4000	4000	4000	4000	4500	4500
16	12	3000	3000	3000	3000	3000	3000	3000	3000	3000	3000	3000	3000	4000
17		SUM(B5;B16)	SUM(C5;C16)	SUM(D5;D16)	SUM(E5;E16)	SUM(F5;F16)	SUM(G5;G16)	SUM(H5;H16)	SUM(I5;I16)	SUM(J5;J16)	SUM(K5;K16)	SUM(L5;L16)	SUM(M5;M16)	SUM(N5;N16)
19	Growth													
20	factor	0,02												
21			B17*(1+B20)	C21*(1+B20)	D21*(1+B20)	E21*(1+B20)	F21*(1+B20)	G21*(1+B20)	H21*(1+B20)	I21*(1+B20)	J21*(1+B20)	K21*(1+B20)	L21*(1+B20)	M21*(1+B20)
23	Smoothing													
24	Factor	0,083	0,166	0,25	0,33	0,417	0,5	0,583	0,666	0,75	0,84	0,91	1	-
26	Revised	1,3												
27	Factor		B17*C24*(1+B26)	C27*C24*(1+B26)	D27*D24*(1+B26)	E27*E24*(1+B26)	F27*F24*(1+B26)	G27*G24*(1+B26)	H27*H24*(1+B26)	I27*I24*(1+B26)	J27*J24*(1+B26)	K27*K24*(1+B26)	L27*L24*(1+B26)	M27*M24*(1+B26)

Fig. A.3 MAT analysis

varying levels of demand. The model provides an easy way of calculating the likely return on capital employed of any particular pricing policy, increasingly important in many companies with budgets based on rates of internal return. The model can also help in the determination of component costing for the finished article. Management can analyse the effect of buying in components against the cost of producing them in-house allowing for all the research and development costs separately from the product cost. The integration of these elements in one complete model (see Fig. A.2) allows the manager to decide (a) the level of capacity that is most profitable to the organization; (b) the most profitable level of volume/base cost/line cost; and (c) the closest approximation to the 'true' cost to the company of any new development.

Forecasting models

Two models are provided. One gives a simple approach to the use of moving annual totals, discussed in the section on forecasting techniques (see Chapter 3), and various smoothing parameters; the other uses regression techniques which enable the manager to determine the interaction of one variable on another and from that to predict the future behaviour of those criteria for forecasting purposes. The use of a moving annual total system (see Fig. A.3) will supply information on gross movements in any particular factor. It may hide important seasonal and non-seasonal trend data. The model allows the manager to introduce a weighting factor into the analysis to make the recent data more important in the trend calculation.

Regression analysis (see Fig. A.4) demands that the variables chosen do, in fact, bear some relation to each other: otherwise the result may produce a correlation which does not in fact exist. Thus there may be a surface correlation between the number of red-headed children and the number of computers sold during the Christmas period. It however would be an unwise firm that based future sales on the production of red-headed children! Often such a correlation will arrive from the lack of data that is correlated, as spurious results will more likely appear from small data sets. Other problems can occur in other areas. When the two factors are interactive the results cannot be trusted as the result of one set of data is dependent on another creating a loop which needs to be broken before reliable output can be achieved. This is also true when the factors are practically identical. The number of cars on the roads and the number of car registrations would be an example in point. To enable the procedure to be most effective a number of precautionary preliminary steps need to be taken with the data:

A/B	C	D	E	F	G	H
2 Regression	Analysis					
6	X-data	X2	Y-data	Y2	X*Y	(X-Y)2
8	15	C8*C8	23	E8*E8	C8*E8	C8-E8*(C8-E8)
9	16	C9*C9	24	E9*E9	C9*E9	C9-E9*(C9-E9)
10	17	C10*C10	27	E10*E10	C10*E10	C10-E10*(C10-E10)
11	19	C11*C11	28	E11*E11	C11*E11	C11-E11*(C11-E11)
12	23	C12*C12	32	E12*E12	C12*E12	C12-E12*(C12-E12)
13	18	C13*C13	23	E13*E13	C13*E13	C13-E13*(C13-E13)
14	19	C14*C14	34	E14*E14	C14*E14	C14-E14*(C14-E14)
15	21	C15*C15	40	E15*E15	C15*E15	C15-E15*(C15-E15)
16	22	C16*C16	45	E16*E16	C16*E16	C16-E16*(C16-E16)
17	13	C17*C17	18	E17*E17	C17*E17	C17-E17*(C17-E17)
18	17	C18*C18	25	E18*E18	C18*E18	C18-E18*(C18-E18)
19	15	C19*C19	26	E19*E19	C19*E19	C19-E19*(C19-E19)
20	18	C20*C20	25	E20*E20	C20*E20	C20-E20*(C20-E20)
21	16	C21*C21	32	E21*E21	C21*E21	C21-E21*(C21-E21)
22	17	C22*C22	59	E22*E22	C22*E22	C22-E22*(C22-E22)
24	SUM(C8;C22)	SUM(D8;D22)	SUM(E8;E22)	SUM(F8;F22)	SUM(G8;G22)	SUM(H8;H22)/13
26	G24-C24*E24/15	D24-C24*C24/15	C26/D26			
28	H24/D26	SQ.RT(C28)	E26/D28			
30 Correlation Factor		E28				

Fig. A.4 Regression analysis

1. Identify and smooth out any major seasonal trend in the data.
2. Identify the logical variables for analysis and then initially graph the relationships to ensure that the variables are independent (disposable income and car ownership would in this context be classified as independent variables, car ownership and car registration would not).
3. Convert variables into their necessary form, and perform the regression equations.
4. Test for predictability.

The model deals with the case where one data set is additional to another in a relationship such as: X=y1+y2+y3. X could be a factor such as sales or demand; y1 would be the base level of demand without the existence of y2 and y3 which could be per capita income factors or ownership of video recorders for example. It can be seen that what the model is attempting to do is to explain a particular factor in respect of the underlying variables that are responsible for the change that is observable over time.

What is derived from the use of regression equations is the identification of possible factors that explain the variation over time of the main variable, such as sales, that the organization wishes to identify. The nature of the information provided can be used to determine whether these relationships are significant or not. From that the model can be used to investigate factors which have a greater level of significance or to use the system to predict values in 'what-if' simulations.

The data sources for use in the model remain an important problem area that most firms need to overcome so that the underlying causal relationships can be explored fully. Such considerations again underly the value of the model in the development of control systems within the firm to collect and analyse relevant data.

Cash flow, profit and loss, balance sheet model

The model (see Fig. A.5) is designed for the small business to enable it to see how cash flow, profit and loss and the balance sheet has changed over the previous two years, and how the funding requirements of the business will change over the forecast and future years as the business grows.

Columns D and E refer to the previous experience of the company. Here the actual results of previous years' trading should be entered so that the forecast can be directly compared with the actual out-turn in previous years, an important factor in deciding whether the plan is in fact realistic or not. Columns U and V refer to the future two years after the forecast year so that the business can see how the forecast relates both to what has previously occurred and what is planned for the future.

cols A- G lines 1-74

	A/B	C	D	E	F	G
1			Yr 2	Lst Yr	Forecast	Rv. Fcst
2						
5						
7	Seasonal Pattern					
8	Net Sales					
10	Cash Receipts					
11	% 30					SUM(H11:S11)
12	% 60					SUM(H12:S12)
13	% 90					SUM(H13:S13)
14	Other Cash Receipts					SUM(H14:S14)
16	Total Cash Inflow					SUM(G11:G14)
18	Labour/Materials					SUM(H18:S18)
19	Admin					SUM(H19:S19)
20	Selling Expenses					SUM(H20:S20)
21	Interest Expense					SUM(H21:S21)
22	Other Expense					SUM(H22:S22)
23	Excpt Exp				SUM(H23:S23)	SUM(H23:S23)
24	Rnt/Rate					SUM(H24:S24)
26	Total Cash Outflow					SUM(G18:G24)
28	Net Cash Outflow				F16-F26	G16-G26
30	Opening Cash					
31						S31
32	Loans Required					
34	P&L					
36	Net Sales					SUM(H36:S36)
37	Cost of Goods Sold					SUM(H37:S37)
39	Gross Profit					SUM(H39:S39)
41	Gen & Admin Exp					SUM(H41:S41)
42	Selling Expenses					SUM(H42:S42)
43	Depreciation					F43
45	Sales Income					SUM(H45:S45)
46	Other Income					SUM(H46:S46)
47	Interest Expense					SUM(H47:S47)
48	Other Expense					SUM(H48:S48)
50	Income before Tax					SUM(H50:S50)
51	Tax Rate					SUM(H51:S51)
53	Net Income					SUM(H53:S53)
55	Balance Sheet					
57	Assets					
59	Current Assets					
60	Cash					
61	Debtors					
62	Stocks					
63	Prepaid Expenses					
65	Total		SUM(D60:D63)	SUM(E60:E63)	SUM(F60:F63)	
67	Fixed Assets					
68	Plant & Equipment					
69	Depreciation					
70	Land					
72	Total Fixed Assets		D68-D69+D70	E68-E69+E70	F68-F69+F70	
74	Total Assets		D65+D72	E65+E72	F65+F72	

Fig. A.5 Cash flow, profit and loss, balance sheet model

cols H- L lines 1-53

	H	I	J	K	L
	Month				
	1	2	3	4	5
	G8*H7/100	G8*I7/100	G8*J7/100	G8*K7/100	G8*L7/100
10					
11	S7/100*E8*E11/100	H8*F11/100	I8*F11/100	J8*F11/100	K8*F11/100
12	R7/100*E8*E11/100	S7/100*F8*F12/100	H8*F12/100	I8*F12/100	J8*F12/100
13	Q7/100*E8*E13/100	R7/100*F8*F13/100	R7/100*F8*F13/100	H8*F13/100	I8*F13/100
14					
16	SUM(H11:H14)	SUM(I11:I14)	SUM(J11:J14)	SUM(K11:K14)	SUM(L11:L14)
18	H8*F18/100	I8*F18/100	J8*F18/100	K8*F18/100	L8*F18/100
19	H8*F19/100	I8*F19/100	J8*F19/100	K8*F19/100	L8*F19/100
20	H8*F20/100	I8*F20/100	J8*F20/100	K8*F20/100	L8*F20/100
21	H32*F21/100	I32*F21/100	J32*F21/100	K32*F21/100	L32*F21/100
22	F22/12	F22/12	F22/12	F22/12	F22/12
23					
24					
26	SUM(H18:H24)	SUM(I18:I24)	SUM(J18:J24)	SUM(K18:K24)	SUM(L18:L24)
28	H16-H26	I16-I26	J16-J26	K16-K26	L16-L26
30	F30	H31	I31	J31	K31
31	H28+H30	I28+I30	J28+J30	K28+K30	L28+L30
32	IFH31>0THEN0ELSE-H31	IFI31>0THEN0ELSE-I31	IFJ31>0THEN0ELSE-J31	IFK31>0THEN0ELSE-K31	IFL31>0THEN0ELSE-L31
34					
36	H8	I8	J8	K8	L8
37	H18	I18	J18	K18	L18
39	H36-H37	I36-I37	J36-J37	K36-K37	L36-L37
41	H19	I19	J19	K19	L19
42	H20+H22	I20+I22	J20+J22	K20+K22	L20+L22
43	F43/12	F43/12	F43/12	F43/12	F43/12
45	H39-SUM(H41:H43)	I39-SUM(I41:I43)	J39-SUM(J41:J43)	K39-SUM(K41:K43)	L39-SUM(L41:L43)
46					
47	H21	I21	J21	K21	L21
48	H23+H24	I23+I24	J23+J24	K23+K24	L23+L24
50	H45+H46-(H47+H48)	I45+I46-(I47+I48)	J45+J46-(J47+J48)	K45+K46-(K47+K48)	L45+L46-(L47+L48)
51					
53	H50-H51	I50-I51	J50-J51	K50-K51	L50-L51

cols M - Q lines 1-53

	M	N	O	P	Q
1					
2					
5	6	7	8	9	10
7					
8	G8*M7/100	G8*N7/100	G8*O7/100	G8*P7/100	G8*Q7/100
10					
11	L8*F11/100	M8*F11/100	N8*F11/100	O8*F11/100	P8*F11/100
12	K8*F12/100	L8*F12/100	M8*F12/100	N8*F12/100	O8*F12/100
13	J8*F13/100	K8*F13/100	L8*F13/100	M8*F13/100	N8*F13/100
14					
16	SUM(M11:M14)	SUM(N11:N14)	SUM(O11:O14)	SUM(P11:P14)	SUM(Q11:Q14)
18	M8*F18/100	N8*F18/100	O8*F18/100	P8*F18/100	Q8*F18/100
19	M8*F19/100	N8*F19/100	O8*F19/100	P8*F19/100	Q8*F19/100
20	M8*F20/100	N8*F20/100	O8*F20/100	P8*F20/100	Q8*F20/100
21	M32*F21/100	N32*F21/100	O32*F21/100	P32*F21/100	Q32*F21/100
22	F22/12	F22/12	F22/12	F22/12	F22/12
23					
24					
26	SUM(M18:M24)	SUM(N18:N24)	SUM(O18:O24)	SUM(P18:P24)	SUM(Q18:Q24)
28	M16-M26	N16-N26	O16-O26	P16-P26	Q16-Q26
30	L31	M31	N31	O31	P31
31	M28+M30	N28+N30	O28+O30	P28+P30	Q28+Q30
32	IFM31>0THEN0ELSE-M31	IFN31>0THEN0ELSE-N31	IFO31>0THEN0ELSE-O31	IFP31>0THEN0ELSE-P31	IFQ31>0THEN0ELSE-Q31
34					
36	M8	N8	O8	P8	Q8
37	M18	N18	O18	P18	Q18
39	M36-M37	N36-N37	O36-O37	P36-P37	Q36-Q37
41	M19	N19	O19	P19	Q19
42	M20+M22	N20+N22	O20+O22	P20+P22	Q20+Q22
43	F43/12	F43/12	F43/12	F43/12	F43/12
45	M39-SUM(M41:M43)	N39-SUM(N41:N43)	O39-SUM(O41:O43)	P39-SUM(P41:P43)	Q39-SUM(Q41:Q43)
46					
47	M21	N21	O21	P21	Q21
48	M23+M24	N23+N24	O23+O24	P23+P24	Q23+Q24
50	M45+M46-(M47+M48)	N45+N46-(N47+N48)	O45+O46-(O47+O48)	P45+P46-(P47+P48)	Q45+Q46-(Q47+Q48)
51					
53	M50-M51	N50-N51	O50-O51	P50-P51	Q50-Q51

cols R - V lines 1-53

	R	S	T	U	V
1				Yr 2+	Yr 3+
2			Grwth		
5	11	12			10
7					
8	G8*R7/100	G8*S7/100		G8*(1+U2/100)	U8*(1+V2/100)
10					
11	Q8*F11/100	R8*F11/100		G11*(1+U2/100)	U11*(1+V2/100)
12	P8*F12/100	Q8*F12/100		G12*(1+U2/100)	U12*(1+V2/100)
13	O8*F13/100	P8*F13/100		G13*(1+U2/100)	U13*(1+V2/100)
14					
16	SUM(R11:R14)	SUM(S11:S14)		G16*(1+U2/100)	U16*(1+V2/100)
18	R8*F18/100	S8*F18/100		G18*(1+U2/100)	U18*(1+V2/100)
19	R8*F19/100	S8*F19/100		G19*(1+U2/100)	U19*(1+V2/100)
20	R8*F20/100	S8*F20/100		G20*(1+U2/100)	U20*(1+V2/100)
21	R32*F21/100	S32*F21/100		G21*(1+U2/100)	U21*(1+V2/100)
22	F22/12	F22/12		G22*(1+U2/100)	U22*(1+V2/100)
23					
24					
26	SUM(R18:R24)	SUM(S18:S24)		G26*(1+U2/100)	U26*(1+V2/100)
28	R16-R26	S16-S26		G28*(1+U2/100)	U28*(1+V2/100)
30	Q31	R31		G30*(1+U2/100)	U30*(1+V2/100)
31	R28+R30	S28+S30		G31*(1+U2/100)	U31*(1+V2/100)
32	IFR31>0THEN0ELSE-R31	IFS31>0THEN0ELSE-S31		G32*(1+U2/100)	U32*(1+V2/100)
34					
36	R8	S8		G36*(1+U2/100)	U36*(1+V2/100)
37	R18	S18		G37*(1+U2/100)	U37*(1+V2/100)
39	R36-R37	S36-S37		G39*(1+U2/100)	U39*(1+V2/100)
41	R19	S19		G41*(1+U2/100)	U41*(1+V2/100)
42	R20+R22	S20+S22		G42*(1+U2/100)	U42*(1+V2/100)
43	F43/12	F43/12		G43*(1+U2/100)	U43*(1+V2/100)
45	R39-SUM(R41:R43)	S39-SUM(S41:S43)		G45*(1+U2/100)	U45*(1+V2/100)
46					
47	R21	S21		G47*(1+U2/100)	U47*(1+V2/100)
48	R23+R24	S23+S24		G48*(1+U2/100)	U48*(1+V2/100)
50	R45+R46-(R47+R48)	S45+S46-(S47+S48)		G50*(1+U2/100)	U50*(1+V2/100)
51					
53	R50-R51	S50-S51		G53*(1+U2/100)	U53*(1+V2/100)

cols A- G lines 76-107

A/B	C	D	E	F	G
76 Liabilities					
78 Current					
79 Creditors					
80 Other Liabilities					
83 Total		D79+D80	E79+E80	F79+F80	
85 Long Term Debt					
87 Total Liabilities		D83+D85	E83+E85	F83+F85	
89 Equity					
90 Shares					
91 Retained Earnings					
93 Total		D90+D91	E90+E91	F90+F91	
95 Total Equity and Liability		D87+D93	E87+E93	F87+F93	
96 ROCE		(D45+D46)/(D90+91/100)	(E45+E46)/(E90+91/100)	(F45+F46)/(F90+91/100)	(G45+G46)/(G90+91/100)
97 GDAFI		D39/D8/100	E39/E8/100	F39/F8/100	G39/G8/100
98 Net Prof		D50/D8/100	E50/E8/100	F50/F8/100	G50/G8/100
99 SER		D20/D8/100	E20/E8/100	F20/F8/100	G20/G8/100
100 AER		D19/D8/100	E19/E8/100	F19/F8/100	G19/G8/100
101 WCR		D65-D83/D8/100	E65-E83/E8/100	F65-F83/F8/100	G65-G83/G8/100
102 STR		D8/D62	E8/E62	F8/F62	G8/G62
103 LCG		D61/D8/365	E61/E8/365	F61/F8/365	G61/G8/365
104 LCT		D79/D18/365	E79/E18/365	F79/F18/365	G79/G18/365
105 CR		D65/D83	E65/E83	F65/F83	G65/G83
106 QA		D65-D62/D83	E65-E62/E83	F65-F62/F83	G65-G62/G83
107 DER		D85/D93	E85/E93	F85/F93	G85/G93

Each month of the forecast year is given a number from 1 to 12 to enable the company to define problems on a month-by-month basis and to consider how changes in the forecast may affect the cash flow or profit later in the year.

The model considers the following factors, relating to cash flow, the profit and loss account and the balance sheet.

Cash flow

1. *Seasonality of trading.* Most companies have differing patterns of sales. The model allows the company, from past history, to enter the relevant seasonality pattern as a percentage of annual sales on a month-by-month basis over the year (line 7).

2. *Forecast monthly sales.* The model calculates the expected monthly sales from the total expected turnover allowing for the seasonality provided by the company. As the year proceeds the actual figure on a month-by-month basis can be entered under the relevant month (line 8). This will provide the company with a continually updated sales forecast in cell G8 which can be compared with the original forecast in cell F8. This provides the company with a valuable method of maintaining management control by continually updating the forecast. Naturally any user of the model would be advised to print out the results on a month-by-month basis and save the monthly record on disk.

3. *Cash receipts.* The way in which money comes into the company will depend on the length of credit that the company is obliged to give. The model takes either the forecast or actual sales figures and, working on the length of credit provided, will break down the cash inflow over the following months. It also takes account of sales prior to the start of the forecast year by applying the seasonality to the total sales of the previous year and deriving the likely cash receipts from this figure for the first three months of the forecast year. The company can also enter other monies that it receives on an irregular basis.

4. *Total cash inflow.* The model will then calculate (line 16) the total amount of money that the company should expect on a month-by-month basis. This provides additional valuable management control information. Should the amount of money actually received by the company be less in any one month than expected there may be problems in credit control which need solution (provided of course that the level of expected sales is being achieved).

5. *Cost of production.* Labour, raw materials, general and administrative costs are entered as percentages of the final selling price. Thus raw materials may account for 60%, labour 10% and so on of the planned selling price. The marginal profitability model will act as an additional

valuable management control technique for this area of business activity. Most important for the business is to monitor the production process continually in order to ensure that the forecast level of costs is being achieved. Changing the percentage allocated will allow the company to re-estimate the forecast profitability. This will also be necessary if the product mix that the company sells changes during the year with a consequent change in the overall profitability of sales: the company will be able to re-calculate the effects on company progress. Should the company wish, it can consider integrating the marginal profitability model with the cash flow model to interrelate the product-by-product analysis with the overall level of company sales and profitability.

6. *Interest expense.* The model will automatically calculate the amount of interest that is owed on the money that the company needs to borrow to balance its cash flow. The amount is calculated from the current interest rate payable on loans by the company. Changing the level of interest rates will enable the company to explore the effects of changing interest rates upon the overall profitability of the operation.

7. *Other expense.* The model allows the company to enter figures for additional expenditure and rent and rates across the year.

8. *Opening and closing cash balances.* The model will calculate the opening and closing cash balances on a month-by-month basis starting from the amount of cash outstanding at the end of the year. It will automatically compare the revised forecast figure with that of the original forecast allowing management to identify problems of cash management that may be developing and enabling them to raise additional finance in ample time to meet a prospective gap in the cash flow.

9. *Loans required.* The model will automatically calculate the level of loans that the company will need to maintain solvency.

The model does not consider the affects of either National Insurance or VAT – it assumes that these will be paid when due.

Profit and loss account

10. *Gross profit.* The level of gross profit will be calculated by the model and can be compared with the forecast level of gross profit and the performance in previous years. Serious divergence from the forecast will mean that the company will have to consider carefully whether the product mix is changing or the level of discounts is too high.

11. *Depreciation.* The model will automatically allocate depreciation costs to each month based on the level of depreciation decided on by the company during the planning process. This figure can be changed should the depreciation policy be altered.

12. Taxes. The model will calculate the amount of taxes that the business will need to pay based on the relevant tax percentage which can be entered in cell C51. The payment is assumed to be made in two instalments in month 6 and month 12.

The model does not consider the issue of dividends, as this will not be often relevant to the small company. However the Spreadsheet can be easily modified if they are considered to be an important funding issue.

Balance sheet

13. Ratios. The company is able to compare the past two years with the current year and the two future years with the key ratios mentioned in Chapter 6.

Index